Contents

Examples

Tables

Chapter 1
Irish Travellers: Background

1.1 Introduction

This chapter provides a brief background on Irish Travellers, their education, accommodation, health, and other challenges facing them, and sets out the format of this report.

1.2 The Traveller community

Irish Travellers are an indigenous minority who, according to historical evidence, have been part of Irish society for centuries. They have a long shared history, value system, language, customs and traditions that make them a group recognised by themselves and others as distinct. This distinctive life-style and culture, based on a nomadic tradition, sets them apart from the settled population. The history of the Traveller community includes a struggle to uphold their distinct cultural identity and to maintain a nomadic way of life. For the purposes of this report it is accepted that Travellers have shared a nomadic tradition and a means of communication, beliefs, values and practices distinct from the majority culture.

The 2002 census of population counted close to 24,000 Travellers. Traveller representatives have expressed concern that the census figure may be an underestimate and suggest that the real figure is approximately 30,000. Some may not have wished to identify themselves as Travellers. (This was the first time such information was sought in the census. Previous censuses had relied on enumerators identifying Travellers who lived in halting-sites, while those in local authority housing were not counted as Travellers.)

The 2002 census found that almost two-thirds of the 7,000 Travellers who gave the age at which their full-time education ceased had left before the then statutory minimum age of fifteen, compared with 15 per cent for the population as a whole. Historically, Travellers were often marginalised in the education system. Into the 1990s Travellers were often educated through segregated provision. Over the last decade this segregated approach has mainly been abandoned in favour of age-appropriate, integrated and inclusive provision.

Travellers are acknowledged in many reports as one of the most marginalised groups in Irish society. This is particularly emphasised, for example, in the *Report of the Task Force on the Travelling Community* (1995). Many Travellers fare poorly on every indicator used to measure disadvantage, including educational attainment, health status, unemployment, poverty, social exclusion, life expectancy, infant mortality, gender equality, political representation, accommodation, and living conditions.

Travellers, like the settled population, are not a homogeneous group. There are Travellers who, because of their sex, sexual orientation, age, disability etc. have complex needs and may experience multiple forms of discrimination. A number of Travellers have broken out of the cycle of material poverty, and some, though a very small number, are participating in, and deriving benefit from, the education system to a high level.

A study by the Economic and Social Research Institute, *Population Structure and Living Circumstances of Irish Travellers* (1986), found that the age structure of Traveller families was radically different from that of the settled population. Among Travellers there was a relatively large number of infants and children and a relatively small number of older people, as a result of a high birth rate and low life expectancy. In 2002 the census found a similar age profile, showing that Travellers are continuing to die younger than their settled peers. It found that the average age of Travellers is eighteen, compared with an average age of thirty-two for the general population. The census also found that 73 per cent of Traveller men and 64 per cent of Traveller women were unemployed, whereas only 4.4 per cent of the total population were unemployed.

1.3 Traveller accommodation

At the end of 2004 the Department of the Environment, Heritage and Local Government evaluated existing Traveller accommodation. This is summarised in table 1.

Table 1: Traveller accommodation, 2004

Types of accommodation	Number of families
Tenants in permanent accommodation provided by, or with the assistance of, local authorities	4,528
Tenants in private rented accommodation	486
Own accommodation from own resources	464
Basic service bays or sharing accommodation	912
Living in unauthorised sites	601
Total	**6,991**

The number of families living on unauthorised sites is declining. In 2002 more than 900 families were living on unauthorised sites. On the other hand, the number living in basic service bays or in shared accommodation has increased from 698 in 2002 to 912 in 2004. One in five Traveller families are living in basic service bays, sharing accommodation, or on unauthorised sites. The quality of accommodation varies greatly, and for those living on unauthorised sites (601 families) there is the constant threat of eviction without notice under section 10 of the Housing (Traveller Accommodation) Act (1998) and the Housing (Miscellaneous Provisions) Act (2002). As a result, many Travellers are living in conditions that are unacceptable with regard to their general well-being and specifically their education. Poor accommodation militates against their being able to participate in a meaningful and productive manner in the education system.

New Traveller accommodation policies are being adopted by local authorities to cover the period 2005-08. It is expected that these schemes will continue to address the accommodation needs of Travellers. In 2005, €45 million was allocated to accommodation specifically for Travellers.

1.4 Traveller health

Travellers are particularly disadvantaged in terms of health status and access to health services. Generally speaking, they suffer poor health on a level which compares so unfavourably with the settled community that it would probably be unacceptable to any section thereof. (*Traveller Health: A National Strategy, 2002-2005, 2002,* section 1.8.)

Travellers of all ages have much higher mortality rates than people in the general population. The infant mortality rate (per 1,000 live births) is nearly three times that of the national population, and Travellers have a life expectancy that is ten years less for men and twelve years less for women. High levels of morbidity and frequent hospitalisation are factors common to Traveller children and to many Travellers generally. The Department of Health and Children's publication *Traveller Health: A National Strategy, 2002-2005* (2002) sets out a clear and practical response to inequities. A Traveller Health Advisory Committee has been established by the department, as has a Traveller Health Unit in each Health Service Executive area. The involvement of Travellers themselves in the provision of health services is considered crucial in bridging the gap between the Traveller community and the health service.

1.5 Discrimination

In addition to the factors described above, the experience and the fear of discrimination dominate the lives of many Travellers. These add a significant level of stress to many aspects of their lives and particularly to their relations with the majority population. The United Nations International Convention on the Elimination of

All Forms of Racial Discrimination (1965) defines racial discrimination as follows:

Any distinction, exclusion, restriction, or preference based on race, colour, descent, or national or ethnic origin which has the purpose or effect of nullifying or impairing the recognition, enjoyment, or exercise, on equal footing, of human rights and fundamental freedoms in the political, economic, social, cultural, or any other field of public life.

The *National Action Plan Against Racism* (2005) sets out the Government's strategy for addressing racism. The general aim of the plan is "to provide strategic direction to combat racism and to develop a more inclusive, intercultural society in Ireland based on a commitment to inclusion by design, not as an add-on or afterthought and based on policies that promote interaction, equality of opportunity, understanding and respect."

1.6 The future

From a Traveller viewpoint, the implications of the scenario described above are serious. It suggests a population in which many are experiencing economic poverty, poor health, exclusion, or an unacceptable educational outcome. From a Government viewpoint, much work is being done to ensure that the lives of Travellers are improved and continue to improve throughout the full spectrum of available services. The implementation of the recommendations in the *Report of the Task Force on the Travelling Community* (1995) is helping to guide such improvements. This report makes recommendations that should improve the lives of Travellers, particularly with regard to education.

1.7 Structure of the report

This report can be divided into two main parts. Chapters 1-3 outline the background, provide the scope and terms of reference, describe the core values and guiding principles of the strategy, explain what a policy of inclusion means, and summarise provision in 2005. Chapters 4-10 set out the background and propose general objectives, recommendations, plans of action, a time scale and expected outcomes with regard to

- parents
- pre-schools
- primary education
- post-primary education
- further education
- higher education
- other educational issues.

The report does contain an element of duplication. For example, some of the topics considered in the chapter on primary education are also considered in the chapter on post-primary education. However, this approach is taken because some readers may be interested in reading only the chapters that are relevant to their sector.

The final chapter provides a holistic context for the report and restates the general objectives, recommendations, and some specific targets and outcomes, summarises generic themes that are found throughout the report, and outlines the future envisaged for Traveller education. The suggested time scale is divided into three categories. A short time span means within two years, a medium span is three to five years, and a long-term span is more than five years. Subject to ministerial acceptance of the recommendations, it is envisaged that an implementation plan will be prepared to activate the strategy.

Many of the views expressed in this report could be directly related to other minority groups, such as people with disabilities. However, for this exercise the report refers only to Travellers, with few references to other disadvantaged groups.

The report contains a number of abbreviations. A glossary of the abbreviations used is given in appendix 1.

A number of references have been used in developing this report, and these are listed at the end of the document.

Chapter 2
Scope and terms of reference, core
values, principles and policy on inclusion

2.1 Introduction

This chapter sets out the scope and terms of reference, core values, and principles, and specifies what is meant by a policy of inclusion.

2.2 Scope and terms of reference

2.2.1 Task Force on the Travelling Community

The Report of the Task Force on the Travelling Community (1995) made 167 recommendations in the field of Traveller education and training - that is, more than half the total number of recommendations. This is a reflection of the complexity of the provision of an education service, from early years to adult and from formal schooling to youth work. The number of recommendations is also a measure of the challenges facing those responsible for, or with an interest in, the promotion of Traveller education.

It is more than ten years since the task force began its deliberations. In 2000 the *First Progress Report of the Committee to Monitor and Co-ordinate the Implementation of the Recommendations of the Task Force on the Travelling Community* was published. The second progress report was published in December 2005. These reports directly address the education recommendations in the 1995 report, taking into account developments that have taken place in the intervening ten years.

Continuity and cohesion throughout the various areas of responsibility are necessary to maximise the benefits to Travellers from the education system. It is necessary to ensure that the highest standards of practice are implemented in an efficient and effective manner, and that value for money is provided. The development and implementation of a strategy has the potential to achieve maximum benefit to Travellers.

A Joint Working Group, consisting of members of the Advisory Committee on Traveller Education and the Educational Disadvantage Committee, was established in November 2003 to provide recommendations for a Traveller education strategy. This report will address short-term, medium-term and long-term goals in all aspects of Traveller education. An external expert was appointed to chair the group and to lead the process. A high-level official of the Department of Education and Science was appointed to assist with the development of the report, and the process was also supported by an expert with a Traveller equality background. (The membership of the Joint Working Group is given in appendix 2 and of the ACTE in appendix 3.)

The aim for Traveller education is to strive to achieve equality of access, equality of participation and equality of outcome for Travellers from education in the context of lifelong learning. This report sets out a way forward in relation to Traveller education, taking account of the complexity of the issues involved, the history of provision, and the existing measures. It sets out the challenges for the future and identifies ways in which to approach those challenges.

There are precedents for the development of such specifically direct, targeted strategies within the education system, for example in the areas of lifelong learning and early-years education. There is also a precedent for such initiatives in the Department of Health and Children, which flows directly from the Task Force Report, *Traveller Health: A National Strategy, 2002-2005* (2002).

2.2.2 Terms of reference
This report:

- examines existing provision and supports and existing organisational and management structures for Traveller education at all levels and makes recommendations for change, as appropriate.

  A review of the present situation in relation to Traveller education - expenditure, issues, problems, challenges, and opportunities - was undertaken.

- identifies clear goals for Traveller education, states objectives, makes recommendations with a series of short-term, medium-term and long-term action plans, and sets out an expected outcome for each sector

- makes recommendations in relation to optimising or reallocating existing resources.

  This will form a central part of the strategy, and the recommendations will also seek to ensure that available resources give priority to those most in need.

- is holistic and seeks to address all aspects of Traveller education for lifelong learning, i.e. from pre-school to adult and continuing education

- included a detailed consultation process.

To inform the Joint Working Group, experienced practitioners from a wide range of relevant areas made presentations to the group. Reports written on different aspects of Traveller education have been considered, including the *National Evaluation Report on Pre-Schools for Travellers* (2003), *Guidelines on Traveller Education in Primary Schools* (2002), and *Guidelines on Traveller Education in Second-Level Schools* (2002). The

Inspectorate of the Department of Education and Science carried out a survey of Traveller education provision, and the Joint Working Group was briefed on the findings of this survey. (The report of this survey was published in May 2006). More than forty public submissions have been received, including a Report on the Consultations with Traveller Learners and Parents, which presents the findings of six consultation seminars (five regional and one national). These six seminars were arranged by Traveller organisations. Appendix 4 lists the organisations and individuals who submitted their views.

This report was prepared by the Joint Working Group and submitted to the Advisory Committee on Traveller Education (ACTE) for comment.

2.3 Core values and guiding principles

There is little doubt regarding the potential value that improvements in Traveller education can have for the whole Traveller community and for society in general. While many factors contribute to the poor living conditions and quality of life of the Traveller community, the improvement in the educational status of Travellers has nevertheless the potential to contribute greatly to the transformation of their general situation and prospects in contemporary Ireland.

With this responsibility in mind, the development of this report was based on the following principles:

1. The report is based on an objective assessment of existing provision, identifies shortcomings, and proposes a way forward. It is based on best practice, drawn from both national and international experience, and on consultations with representatives of the partners involved.

2. It is clear that best practice requires that due regard be given to the rights of the child, both as an individual and as a member of their community. The UN Convention on the Rights of the Child (1989) compels us to take account of the child's needs and the child's culture in all aspects of education. It further requires us to ensure that the rights of the child are upheld without discrimination of any kind. This report reflects the "voice of the child" principle as enshrined in the UN Convention on the Rights of the Child (1989) and in the National Children's Office publication *Young Voices* (2005).

3. The report endorses the inclusion of Travellers in the mainstream education system, in a way that respects Travellers' cultural identity, including nomadism.

4. Inclusion in the mainstream will require building the capacity of the mainstream services to deal positively with diversity and not to be predicated on the assumption that all Traveller children and adults have learning difficulties. This will ensure that the mainstream services are accessible, relevant, welcoming, and competent to include Travellers in appropriate ways.

5. All education services should be provided in a way that is equitable and fair and that addresses the danger of racism and discrimination.

6. It is clear from existing evidence that Travellers can experience difficulties in obtaining access to education and training services. This report therefore considers equity in the provision of an education service. This requires an acceptance that equity is based not just on equality of access but on equality of participation and outcome and that the particular needs and culture of Travellers require an innovative approach to planning.

7. The report promotes an intercultural and anti-bias approach to education, recognising the cultural diversity that exists in our country as a welcome strength, to be validated, celebrated and nurtured as a positive resource in our society.

8. The education system is a complex one that involves many different stakeholders. Successful implementation of the recommendations will be challenging and will require an openness to change and the full commitment and participation of all the stakeholders. The active participation of Travellers will be encouraged. The report is based on a commitment to partnership, which recognises the distinct roles, expertise and strengths of each partner. A process will be promoted whereby Travellers and all stakeholders take an active role and a responsibility for successful implementation.

9. There is a need to ensure that all extra measures adopted to support Traveller education avoid creating dependence and isolation. Such measures should, on the other hand, create independence and responsibility and promote interactive and interdependent engagement with the mainstream service. There is a need to set targets, continuously monitor progress, and evaluate outcomes.

10. The report calls for a greater integration, cohesion and co-ordination of services and policy both within the education system and between Government departments and other agencies, thereby enhancing the service provided to Travellers.

11. The report recognises the role of parents as the primary educators and seeks to consult, support and promote the capacity of Traveller parents to effectively execute that role in a concrete manner. In particular, Traveller parents will be enabled to participate fully in the education process and to support their children in remaining in mainstream education as long as possible.

12. The value and importance of consultation with Traveller children on matters relating to their own education is considered an important aspect of the education process.

13. The role and function of all the school community and in particular teachers is of paramount importance in the education process. The contribution made by the school community and the teaching profession to the educational development of the Traveller community is acknowledged, and there have been many success stories. The attitudes and expectations of teachers are crucial for Traveller education. The pre-service, induction and continuing professional development of all teachers should be given the resources to take account of matters relevant to Traveller education. It is imperative that an anti-bias and intercultural dimension form an integral part of and underpin all pre-service, induction and continuing professional development of teachers.

14. The report endorses the contribution and the impact that continuing access to educational opportunities, that is, lifelong learning, can have for adult Travellers, particularly in the light of the low level of formal education they may have experienced. In addition, it endorses the need for consultation with adult Traveller learners on aspects of lifelong learning. Traveller parents with children attending school should be particularly encouraged to become involved in education within the concept of lifelong learning.

2.4 Policy of inclusion

Inclusion is a core principle and a central theme of this report. Based on this principle, it is recommended that all educational provision for Travellers be integrated, in a phased manner, in an enhanced mainstream provision that will result in an inclusive model of educational provision. It is paramount that future education services, therefore, are not provided in a manner that creates new segregation within mainstream provision. This policy will obviously have serious implications, not just for the one remaining special primary school and three junior education centres at post-primary level but also for the forty-five existing Traveller pre-schools and thirty-three senior Traveller training centres, together with three outreach centres in the STTC network.

Changes to be implemented in this regard must be carefully planned, with the best interests of the Traveller learner being paramount throughout. The extensive expertise and good practice that has built up in many of these segregated centres must not be lost but incorporated in mainstream services. The capacity of mainstream services must continue to be built up to deal positively with diversity, thereby ensuring that services provided under the inclusive model will be accessible, welcoming, and have the necessary competence to include Travellers in appropriate ways, respecting their values and culture. A fully inclusive model will take longer than the five-year life span of this report to be fully realised. However, the recommendations in the report can be seen as the impetus towards inclusion in an enhanced mainstream provision.

In certain circumstances it is appropriate to have short to medium-term affirmative action measures to promote equal opportunity so as to allow mainstreaming to become a reality.

For the sake of clarity, "inclusion" in this report encompasses the following:

1. the integration of Travellers in mainstream provision at all levels of the education system, in a fully inclusive model of educational provision, thereby creating a positive environment for all the Traveller community;

2. the provision of resources in accordance with identified educational need;

3. the sharing of the same accommodation and other physical resources by Travellers and settled learners;

4. the inclusion of the reality, needs, aspirations, validation of culture and life experiences of Travellers in planning the curriculum, in educational administration, and in the day-to-day life in each educational setting, including the special education setting;

5. the promotion and acceptance of parity of esteem, whereby difference is acknowledged, respected, and welcomed;

6. the pursuit of ways and means to respond to the educational needs of nomadic Travellers;

7. all components of pre-service, induction and continuing professional development courses to be

informed by the principles of equality, diversity, and inclusion;

All those involved in the education system should have an understanding of anti-discrimination, anti-racism, anti-bias and interculturalism so that all education professionals will have the skills, knowledge and attitudes for dealing with issues and challenges and for making the inclusive school and education system a reality. Within this inclusive context, Traveller identity and culture would be addressed.

8. affirmation and support in education for Travellers with disabilities and also for their parents;

9. the provision of education in a way that accepts and validates the identity of all Traveller learners, including Travellers with disabilities.

2.4.1 Terminology
In this report, where reference is made to an inclusive school or an inclusive education system this is done on the understanding that "inclusive" incorporates equality and diversity together with an understanding of anti-discrimination, anti-racism, anti-bias, and interculturalism.

2.5 Expected outcome

The principle of inclusion has consequences for everyone involved in education, including the Department of Education and Science, policy-makers, teacher educators, school management authorities, teachers' unions, professional organisations, parents' representative bodies, Traveller organisations, parents (both Traveller and settled), school principals, teachers, and pupils. In the implementation of the recommendations the principle of inclusion should continue to become a reality within the full spectrum of the education system, from pre-school to adult education.

Chapter 3
Traveller education, 2005

3.1 Introduction

This chapter outlines the situation with regard to Traveller education in 2005. It provides facts but does not analyse provision, as this is done in the chapters that follow. It looks briefly at general Government policy and refers to international policy, to legislation, and to existing structures. It describes the services, personnel and financial resources available for Traveller education, from pre-school to further education. It also defines intercultural education and describes a team approach to teaching. A brief summary of the Traveller organisations involved in the development of this report is also given.

3.2 Government policy

The *National Action Plan against Poverty and Social Exclusion*, 2001-2003 and 2003-2005, set the principal education targets for Traveller education, including:

- age-appropriate placement of Traveller children in primary schools by 2003

- the transfer rate of Travellers to post-primary schools to be increased to 95 per cent by 2004

- the retention of Traveller pupils to completion of the post-primary senior cycle

- meeting the needs of early school-leavers through Youthreach and STTCs

- providing Travellers with further education and training options

- doubling the participation by mature disadvantaged students in third-level institutions, including Travellers.

National Action Plan against Racism: Planning for Diversity, published by the Department of Justice, Equality and Law Reform in 2005, sets out an intercultural framework for the plan. The components of the framework include **protection, inclusion, provision, recognition,** and **participation.** The implementation of the plan will be through a whole-system approach. A steering group has been established to monitor the implementation of the plan. The Department of Education and Science will continue to promote interculturalism.

3.3 International policy

A number of international conventions and reports affect Ireland's policy relating to Traveller education.

These include:

- Council of Europe Framework Convention for the Protection of National Minorities (1998)

- First National Report by Ireland on the Convention (2001)

- Second National Report by Ireland on the Convention (2005)

- United Nations International Convention on the Elimination of All Forms of Racial Discrimination (1968) - ratified by Ireland in December 2000

- First National Report by Ireland on the Convention (2004).

3.4 Legislation

The principal legislation that affects Traveller education includes:

- the Universities Act (1997), which requires universities to "promote access to the university and to university education by economically or socially disadvantaged people and by people from sections of society significantly under-represented"

- the Education Act (1998), which in its preamble stresses the need to respect the diversity of values, beliefs, languages and traditions in Irish society

The act requires schools to establish and maintain an admission policy that provides for maximum accessibility to the school. Section 29 allows for appeals to the Secretary-General of the Department of Education and Science where, for example, the board of a school refuses to enrol a pupil in that school. In addition, schools are required to have a school plan that states its objectives relating to equality of access to and participation in the school. This school plan should be available to parents. Section 32 of the act provides for the establishment of the Educational Disadvantage Committee to advise the Minister on policies and strategies to be adopted to identify and correct educational disadvantage

- the Employment Equality Acts (1998 and 2004) and the Equal Status Act (2000) and Equality Act (2004), which identify the nine grounds on which discrimination is prohibited; membership of the Traveller community is one of those grounds

Educational establishments are not, according to section 7 (2) of the Equal Status Act (2000), allowed to discriminate in relation to admission, access to courses and facilities, participation, or expulsion. Section 24 of the 1998 act does allow for positive action on equal opportunities, and this provision is strengthened in the Equality Act (2004), section 15

- the Education (Welfare) Act (2000), which led to the establishment of the National Educational Welfare Board in 2002 as the single national body with responsibility for school attendance

This act provides a comprehensive framework for promoting regular school attendance and for tackling the problems of absenteeism and early school-leaving. The general functions of the NEWB are to ensure that each child attends a recognised school or otherwise receives a certain minimum education.

3.5 Structures and committees

3.5.1 High-Level Group on Traveller Issues
A High-Level Group on Traveller Issues, chaired by the Department of Justice, Equality and Law Reform, has been established at the direction of the Cabinet Committee on Social Inclusion. This group aims to achieve inter-agency co-operation in the co-ordinated provision of services to Travellers. The group reports back to the Cabinet Committee on Social Inclusion. The Department of Education and Science is represented on this group. The report of the group was published in the spring of 2006.

3.5.2 Committee to Monitor and Co-ordinate the Implementation of the Recommendations of the Task Force on the Travelling Community
This committee is chaired by the Department of Justice, Equality and Law Reform. Its object is to monitor the implementation of the recommendations of the *Report of the Task Force on the Travelling Community* (1995) that have been accepted by the Government. The Department of Education and Science, other Government departments and Traveller NGOs are represented on the committee. Its Second Progress Report was published in December 2005.

3.5.3 Equality Authority
The Equality Authority promotes and defends the rights established in the equality legislation and provides leadership on equality issues.

3.5.4 Structures and committees within the Department of Education and Science
Within the Department of Education and Science the provision of education to Travellers is co-ordinated by a high-level official.

- An internal Co-ordinating Committee for Traveller Education had been established in the Department before work on this report began.

- A National Education Officer for Travellers was appointed in 1992. The NEOT identifies the educational needs of Travellers, provides advice on policy and educational provision, and is actively involved in promoting the department's policy on integrated provision. This includes working with schools, designing and providing training, and collecting and collating data. The NEOT works closely with the Visiting Teacher Service for Traveller Education (VTST) and with the high-level official and, with the VTST, provides continuing professional development courses to principals and teachers. The work of the NEOT is described in the *Guidelines on Traveller Education,* which were issued to primary and post-primary schools in 2002.

- An Advisory Committee on Traveller Education (ACTE) was established in 1998 as a direct result of one of the recommendations of the 1995 task force. Membership of the committee is drawn from the main stakeholders in Traveller education. (See appendix 3.)

- The Educational Disadvantage Committee (EDC), established under section 32 of the Education Act (1998), is responsible for addressing broader issues of educational disadvantage, many of which are relevant to Travellers.

In March 2005 the Regional Office Service of the Department of Education and Science took over the responsibility for managing and supporting the Visiting Teacher Service for Travellers.

3.6 Publications

A number of publications deal with issues that are directly or indirectly relevant to the education of Travellers. Many of these are listed at the end of this report.

Delivering Equality of Opportunity in Schools: An Action Plan for Educational Inclusion
The Department of Education and Science published *Delivering Equality of Opportunity in Schools: An Action Plan for Educational Inclusion* (DEIS) in May 2005. The plan provides for a new integrated School Support Programme (SSP) that will bring together and build on existing schemes and initiatives for schools and school communities with a concentrated level of educational disadvantage. The new SSP will include 320 urban and 320 rural primary schools and also 200 post-primary

schools. Support will also continue to be provided for schools in which the level of disadvantage is more dispersed. The plan will be implemented in a phased manner, starting during the school year 2005/06. It is estimated that the schools that are the subject of the SSP will include about 60 per cent of Traveller children. The remaining 40 per cent are enrolled in schools that are not the subject of this plan, but they will be catered for either by existing interventions or by the recommendations in this report.

Survey of Traveller Education Provision

The Inspectorate of the Department of Education and Science undertook a *Survey of Traveller Education Provision* (STEP) in thirty primary and six post-primary schools in 2004. The findings (published in May 2006) have informed the drafting of this report. Some of the findings and recommendations are outlined in chapters 6 and 7 of this report.

3.7 Services, personnel and resources available for Traveller education

3.7.1 Visiting Teacher Service for Travellers

The Visiting Teacher Service for Travellers (VTST) was established in 1980. By 1995 there were eleven VTST posts, but this number has increased significantly, as recommended in the 1995 task force report, which acknowledged that "few initiatives in the area of Traveller education have been as successful as the appointment of visiting teachers." There are now forty visiting teacher posts.

The visiting teachers are based throughout the country and in 2004/05 worked with approximately eight thousand Traveller pupils and their parents. They provide a service that spans the spectrum of the education system, from pre-school to primary and post-primary, and also the transfer to further and higher education. The VTST, through its knowledge, experience and understanding of Travellers and their issues with education, seeks to provide opportunities for Traveller parents, their children and schools to engage in a process of development that maximises participation and attainment levels and promotes a culturally inclusive education for all. Visiting teachers continue to support Traveller parents in obtaining access to education and, where necessary, in dealing with educational exclusion through the legislative process (Education Act (1998), section 29, "Appeals"). Visiting teachers work collaboratively with all the education partners to facilitate the realisation of equality of access, equality of participation, equality of educational status and equality of outcome for Traveller learners.

Since March 2005 the management of the VTST has come under the remit of the Regional Office Service of the Department of Education and Science. Through a partnership model of management, the Regional Office Service plans to give greater support to the VTST in its work. The VTST will continue to identify and give priority to the educational needs of Traveller learners and to collect data on all aspects of levels of participation in Traveller education. The service provided will be enhanced by a more integrated collaboration with all the partners (for example NEWB, NEPS, and NCSE), which the Regional Office Service will facilitate.

3.7.2 Resource teachers for Travellers

Circular 7/99 sets out the procedures for the appointment of resource teachers for Travellers (RTTs). RTT posts are allocated to primary schools to cater for the educational needs of Traveller children of primary-school age. In 2004/05 there were 523 RTT posts throughout the country. One RTT is allocated to a school for each fourteen Traveller pupils enrolled. The school has to seek parental agreement regarding acceptance of the services of a resource teacher in respect of each child.

3.7.3 Home-school-community liaison

The HSCL scheme encourages the involvement of parents, including Traveller parents, in the education of their children and endorses the continuous development of a partnership between the school community and all parents, among other responsibilities. There are approximately 400 co-ordinators serving 500 schools; and in rural areas where "Giving Children an Even Break" applies there are 70 co-ordinators serving approximately 360 schools. Local committees are established that identify school-related issues at the community level that impinge on pupils' attainment.

3.7.4 Pre-schools for Travellers

There are forty-five pre-schools for Travellers throughout the country. In addition, some Traveller children attend community child-care facilities and also Early Start pre-schools. Attendance at pre-school gives the young children a valuable educational experience and prepares them for primary education. The Department of Education and Science carried out a national evaluation of the pre-schools for Travellers, and its report, published in 2003, makes recommendations on how the early-childhood education of very young Travellers can be improved. The report of that evaluation informed the deliberations for this report.

The provision of targeted early-childhood education is a central element of the DEIS Action Plan. This plan will concentrate early-education actions on those children, aged from three up to school enrolment age, who will subsequently attend one of the 180 urban primary schools participating in the SSP and serving the most disadvantaged communities. The extension of early-education support to areas served by other primary schools participating in the SSP will be considered after the initial objective has been achieved.

3.7.5 Primary and post-primary education
Traveller pupils enrolled in both primary and post-primary schools are entitled to the same education as all other pupils and are entitled to learning support and resource support in the same way as other pupils in response to identified educational needs. The *Learning Support Guidelines* published by the Department of Education and Science in 2000 for primary schools promote good practice so that all children may achieve appropriate levels of literacy and numeracy during their primary education.

3.7.6 Primary education
In addition, to assist with the primary education of Traveller children there are a number of special provisions:

- There were 523 resource teachers for Travellers (RTTs) providing additional learning support to Traveller pupils in 2004/05. In some instances the allocation of these RTTs is based on identity rather than educational need.

- An enhanced capitation grant is provided for each Traveller pupil enrolled in a school that has the services of an RTT. There are two capitation rates, one for children under the age of twelve and a higher rate for children over twelve.

- A number of schemes for combating disadvantage exist, including the Home-School-Community Liaison Scheme, the School Completion Programme (SCP), and Giving Children an Even Break.

- *Guidelines on Traveller Education in Primary Schools* (2002) puts forward the department's policy on integration, gives information on Traveller culture, and provides advice and guidance for the management, principals, teachers and parents on responding to the educational needs of Traveller children in an inclusive manner.

- Traveller children have the same entitlements to school transport as other children. Traveller pupils living in halting sites or in other special circumstances are provided with special transport where this is considered necessary. In some instances charitable organisations provide transport, for which 98 per cent grant is payable by the department, with the balance of the cost borne by the charity.

- The publication of the NCCA's *Guidelines on Intercultural Education in the Primary School* in May

2005, together with the *Guidelines on Traveller Education* (2002), provides information and help for schools in increasing their understanding of diversity. The *Guidelines on Intercultural Education* have adopted a cross-curricular, whole-school approach.

- School development planning (SDP) requires primary schools to evaluate the needs of their pupils. All schools have to take account of ethnic and cultural diversity among their pupils and of any particular issues that may arise.

In accordance with the National Anti-Poverty Strategy's objective that the age-appropriate placement of all Travellers in primary schools be achieved by 2003, the best information available, collected annually by the VTST and collated by the NEOT, suggests that almost all Traveller children in primary schools are in age-appropriate classes.

3.7.7 Post-primary education
The transfer rate for Travellers to the post-primary level was 85 per cent in 2004. There were approximately 1,850 Traveller pupils in mainstream post-primary schools, out of a possible 4,000, that is, 46 per cent of all Traveller pupils of post-primary school age. Table 2 gives the estimated number of Traveller pupils in mainstream post-primary schools by school class for 2004/05, as provided by the NEOT.

Table 2: Estimated number of Traveller pupils in mainstream post-primary schools by school class, 2004/05

	Male	Female	Total
First year	303	368	671
Second year	253	303	556
Third year	151	206	357
Transition year or fourth year	14	30	44
Fifth year	47	98	145
Sixth year	25	47	72
Total	**793**	**1,052**	**1,845**

One of the main problems for Traveller pupils is the high drop-out rate from post-primary education, with the majority leaving before completing the junior cycle. There have been some improvements, as can be seen from table 3, which gives the estimated distribution of Traveller pupils in mainstream post-primary schools in recent years as provided by the NEOT.

Table 3: Estimated distribution of Traveller pupils in mainstream post-primary schools in recent years

	1999/2000	2000/01	2001/02	2002/03	2003/04	2004/05
First year	478	531	582	650	626	671
Second year	266	319	397	482	527	556
Third year	116	183	220	272	341	357
Fourth year or transition year	31	27	31	26	44	44
Fifth year	51	67	86	102	113	145
Sixth year	19	38	49	62	63	72
Total	**961**	**1,165**	**1,365**	**1,594**	**1,714**	**1,845**

To assist with the post-primary education of Traveller children there are a number of special provisions:

- Each post-primary school is provided with an additional 1.5 ex-quota teaching hours per week for each Traveller pupil enrolled. This equated to 136 whole-time-equivalent posts in 2004/05.

- A supplementary capitation grant is available for each Traveller pupil enrolled.

- Traveller children have the same entitlements to school transport as other children. Traveller pupils living in halting sites or in other special circumstances are provided with special transport where this is considered necessary. For some, charitable organisations provide transport, for which a 98 per cent grant is payable by the department, with the balance of the cost borne by the charity.

- A number of schemes for combating disadvantage exist, including the HSCL Scheme and the SCP. The SCP discriminates positively by identifying individual children of school-going age who are at risk, both in and out of school, and arranges supports for addressing inequalities in access, participation, and outcome. The scheme includes homework clubs and holiday activities, and its main aim is to retain young people in the formal education system to completion of the senior cycle or equivalent. While approximately 1,300 Traveller children are at present the subject of this initiative in primary and post-primary schools, the SCP is an inclusive and integrated programme, and many whole-school and whole-class supports are offered. The scheme brings together all local stakeholders (home, school, youth, community, statutory, and voluntary) to tackle early school-leaving.

- The National Educational Psychological Service (NEPS) has considered issues relating to the assessment and post-primary placement of Traveller pupils and has reported its findings to the department.

- *Guidelines on Traveller Education in Second-level Schools* (2002) puts forward the department's policy on integration, gives information on Traveller culture, and provides advice on responding to the educational needs of Traveller pupils.

In addition, the implementation of the policy of age-appropriate placement of Traveller pupils is having a positive impact in most post-primary schools. Each post-primary school, through the SDPI, is required to evaluate the needs of its pupils. All schools must take account of ethnic and cultural diversity and any particular issues that may arise. Curricular and programme choice, including the Junior Certificate School Programme and the Leaving Certificate - Applied, make school more relevant to Traveller pupils.

3.8 Financial support for Traveller education

Table 4 shows the financial resources that were expended on Traveller education (above and beyond expenditure on mainstream education) from 1999/2000 to 2004/05.

Table 4: Estimated financial resources expended on Traveller education above and beyond expenditure on mainstream education, 1999/2000-2004/05

	1999/2000	2000/01	2001/02	2002/03	2003/04	2004/05
Pre-schools for Travellers	€1.0m	€1.0m	€1.0m	€1.0m	€1.0m	€0.92m (approx. 500 pupils)
Resource teachers for Travellers at primary level*	€18.4m (460 RTTs)	€19.0m (480 RTTs)	€20.8m (520 RTTs)	€23.4m (520 RTTs)	€26.5m (520 RTTs)	€28.7m (523 RTTs)
Teaching hours, post-primary (whole-time-equivalent posts)	€3.6m (80 WTE posts)	€4m (90 WTE posts)	€4.9m (120 WTE posts)	€5.8m (123 WTE posts)	€6.9m (138 WTE posts)	€7m (136 WTE posts)
Enhanced capitation, primary	€1.4m (5,500 pupils)	€1.5m (5,700 pupils)	€1.5m (5,700 pupils)	€1.55m (5,700 pupils)	€1.6m (5,900 pupils)	€1.77m (approx. 6,000 pupils)
Additional capitation, post-primary	€0.5m (1,200 pupils)	€0.55m (1,300 pupils)	€0.76m (1,600 pupils)	€0.78m (1,700 pupils)	€0.78m (1,700 pupils)	€0.87m (approx. 1,800 pupils)
Visiting Teacher Service for Travellers (40 posts) and National Education Officer for Travellers*	€1.9m	€1.9m	€1.9m	€2.0m	€2.0m	€2.2m
Junior education centres (VECs) - Capitation	€0.04m (4 centres; 175 pupils)	€0.03m	€0.03m (3 centres; 100 pupils)	€0.03m (3 centres; 100 pupils)	€0.03m (3 centres; 80 pupils)	€0.03m (3 centres; 80 pupils)
Senior Traveller training centres	€12.2m	€12.5m	€12.9m	€13m	€13m	€13m (1,098 learners)
Youthreach (pay costs)⁺						(330 learners)
Transport	€0.55m	€0.65m	€0.65m	€0.65m	€0.65m	€0.65m
Salary for education co-ordinator seconded to SSVP to co-ordinate Traveller transport⁺	€0.04m	€0.04m	€0.045m	€0.045m	€0.05m	€0.05m
Total	€39.63m	€41.17m	€44.48m	€47.61m	€52.51m	€55.2m

* The cost of RTTs and VTST is based on a notional salary of €40,000 per annum up to 2002, €45,000 for 2003, €50,000 for 2004, and €55,000 for 2005, to reflect the national pay increases and benchmarking.

⁺ These expenditure figures are based on calendar year rather than school year.

Based on an estimate of approximately 9,800 Traveller learners in the services described above, approximately €5,600 per capita per annum was spent on specific additional supports for Traveller education and training in 2004/05.

3.9 Team approach to teaching

It should not be assumed that all Traveller children require additional educational support. An exclusive reliance on the use of resource hours or resource teachers for individual tuition would be contrary to the principle of integration in teaching and learning. Circular 7/99 of the Department of Education and Science, "Applications for posts of resource teacher for children of the Travelling community," states:

The Department's policy in relation to the education of Traveller children is that they should be taught in an integrated setting. In order to assist with the integration of the Traveller children, a Resource Teacher for Travellers (RTT) post is allocated to primary schools to cater for the educational needs of Traveller children of primary school-going age.

The RTT post is allocated on the understanding that the Traveller children are taught either within their classroom with the RTT working in partnership with their classroom teacher or withdrawn in groups for intensive tuition according to their ages and perceived needs by the RTT.

The circular also states that the school must have confirmation that the school has received parental agreement regarding acceptance of the services of the resource teacher in respect of each child.

Circular 24/03 reinforces this approach. RTTs should liaise with parents to keep them informed of their children's progress and should encourage and develop the parents' involvement. An educational programme should be devised in accordance with perceived needs and informed by the *Learning Support Guidelines* (2000), issued to all schools. The department's Learning Support Guidelines (2000) provide an excellent framework for the planning and provision of supplementary teaching that involves:

• a whole-school approach to learning support

• a collaborative and consultative approach

• the prevention of failure and the provision of intensive early intervention.

While this is department policy, practice in many instances does not reflect policy as described above. The report *Literacy and Numeracy in Disadvantaged Schools: Challenges for Teachers and Learners* (2005) notes that there is limited involvement by classroom teachers in planning to meet the learning needs of pupils.

This programme should be reviewed regularly and at least once a year. Class and support teachers are challenged to work more closely as practices shift from a model of withdrawing children with special educational needs for supplementary teaching to a model of team teaching alongside their peers in the mainstream class. This team approach requires all teachers to work collaboratively and to communicate in order to provide the most effective, appropriate and inclusive education possible for all children. (This is discussed in the STEP report, published in 2006.)

An important theme of the NCCA's consultation on special education considered how teachers plan and work together in the interests of the pupils.

3.10 Intercultural education

The NCCA's *Guidelines on Intercultural Education in the Primary School* (2005) notes that intercultural education has two focal points:

• It is education that respects, celebrates and recognises the normality of diversity in all areas of human life. It sensitises the learner to the idea that humans have naturally developed a range of different ways of life, customs, and world views, and that this breadth of human life enriches all of us.

• It is education that promotes equality and human rights, challenges unfair discrimination, and promotes the values on which equality is built.

Intercultural approaches to education and curriculum are relatively new in schools and require a systematic and concerted effort in order to integrate Travellers fully in the ethos, culture and educational life of schools. This approach is explained in detail in the *Guidelines on Traveller Education in Primary Schools* (2002). In addition, the NCCA's *Guidelines on Intercultural Education in the Primary School* (2005) further reinforces the importance of a whole-school approach, whereby the school changes into the intercultural and inclusive school.

3.11 Special schools for Travellers

There is only one remaining special primary school for Travellers, in Bray, Co. Wicklow. Since June 2004 there are no special classes for Traveller pupils in mainstream schools.

3.12 Junior education centres for Travellers

There are three junior education centres, two in Dublin and one in Athlone, catering for pupils aged between twelve and fifteen. The Department of Education and Science funds these centres. The children are provided with door-to-door transport, breakfast and lunch and are not required to wear a uniform, and their parents are not required to provide any financial support.

3.13 Senior Traveller training centres

There are thirty-three senior Traveller training centres (STTC) throughout the country and three outreach centres. On 31 December 2004, 981 trainees were enrolled in the centres, 799 female and 182 male, aged from fifteen upwards. There is no upper age limit. There were 248 trainees under the age of eighteen, with the majority aged between eighteen and forty-five. The department's policy of having no upper age limit was adopted to attract adults who may previously have had negative experiences of mainstream education and also because of the positive influence this could have on encouraging their children's participation in schooling. These centres provide a programme of general education, vocational training, work experience, and guidance, counselling, and psychological services. A national co-ordinator promotes and monitors the development of the network of STTCs. Trainees are paid a training allowance while attending the centres, and child care is provided to participants.

3.14 Youthreach

In December 2004 a census of Youthreach trainees was taken. There were 2,746 trainees, of whom 330 were Travellers. Youthreach is an integral part of the national programme of second-chance education and training, directed at unemployed early school-leavers aged between fifteen and twenty. It offers participants the opportunity to identify and pursue viable options within adult life and provides them with opportunities to acquire certification. It is a full-time, year-round programme, and child care is provided to participants.

3.15 Access to higher education

In 2004 the National Office for Equity of Access to Higher Education published *Achieving Equity of Access to Higher Education in Ireland: Action Plan, 2005-2007*. The office will set targets for each under-represented group. Travellers are a target group of this plan, which also intends to evaluate existing access schemes so as to develop a national framework of policies, initiatives and successful partnerships to widen access and to support the subsequent participation of all under-represented groups in higher education.

3.16 Traveller Organisations

There are four main Traveller organisations. The first three described below are represented on the Joint Working Group, and all four are represented on the ACTE.

The **National Traveller Women's Forum** was founded in 1988. It is a national network of Traveller women and Traveller organisations that aims to work collectively to challenge discrimination and sexism experienced by Traveller women and to promote Traveller women's right to self-determination and the attainment of human rights and equality within society. It seeks to encourage and support Traveller women in taking up positions and leadership roles within the Traveller community. The forum has also developed and implemented a number of education initiatives, including directly supporting Traveller women's participation in third-level education and providing leadership training to enhance and support Traveller women's participation in decision-making arenas.

The **Irish Traveller Movement** was formed in 1990 to be a campaign through which Travellers and settled people could seek full equality for Travellers in society. The movement challenges the many forms of individual, structural and institutional discrimination that Travellers encounter through a range of strategies, including community development, lobbying and campaigning and also through representation on Government committees and with the wider community and voluntary sector. The ITM is a national Traveller representative organisation, its membership made up of local Traveller groups and organisations. It also includes individual members with an interest in Traveller issues.

Pavee Point is a voluntary organisation that for the last twenty years has been committed to the attainment of human rights for Travellers. It consists of a partnership of Irish Travellers and settled people who work together to address the needs of Travellers and Roma experiencing exclusion and marginalisation and to contribute to improving their quality of life and living circumstances. This work is based on two central premises:

- Travellers need to be actively involved in improving their living and social situation.

- The settled community has a responsibility to address various processes that exclude Travellers from participating as equals in society.

Pavee Point has eight programmes that take innovative approaches to addressing their two main premises.

The **National Association of Travellers' Centres** was founded in 1980 as a voluntary representative association. It is the recognised advisory and lobbying body to the Department of Education and Science and other policy-makers on behalf of all stakeholders participating in senior Traveller training centres. The NATC is also the main provider of Youthwork services to Traveller youths. The general aim of the service is to enable young Travellers between the ages of five and twenty-five, both male and female, to become involved in their leisure and social development and in the development of their own community, both locally and nationally. This is done by providing culturally appropriate projects that meet their identified educational, social, leisure and spiritual needs. (See section 10.2.4 for further details.)

Chapter 4
Traveller parents

4.1 Introduction

This chapter discusses the role of parents and in particular Traveller parents in education. It sets out recommendations and proposed plans of action, with time scales. It describes some of the challenges facing Traveller parents and acknowledges the involvement of Traveller parents in the education system.

4.2 Role of parents

The role of all parents as primary educators is recognised in the Constitution of Ireland and is of crucial importance in children's education. While the responsibilities of Traveller parents in the education process is acknowledged, their capacity to engage in the process is determined by several factors, one of the most significant being their own educational and socio-economic background. The role of the Department of Education and Science and of all providers of education in involving Traveller parents is also crucial. Many demands face every parent of school-going children, and meeting these demands in any environment is challenging. Parents are expected to be able to deal with a whole range of educational issues, such as:

• choice of school

• the process of enrolment

• continuous liaison with the school

• monitoring educational progress

• promoting an interest in reading

• helping with homework

• providing the resources needed to meet a child's educational needs

• providing resources for the extracurricular activities of their children

• dealing with difficulties as they arise

• creating a stimulating, supportive and pro-education home environment that will lead to lifelong learning.

4.3 Challenges for Traveller parents

Many additional challenges face Traveller parents, above and beyond those facing most settled parents. Their situation has a number of distinct and identifiable

characteristics that make it more difficult for Traveller parents generally to provide the type of support and environment required. Approximately 9 per cent of Traveller families are living in unauthorised sites, and the reality of living without access to basic services and being under possible threat of eviction without notice under section 10 of the Housing (Traveller Accommodation) Act (1998) and the Housing (Miscellaneous Provisions) Act (2002) has the potential of affecting a Traveller child's education in a very negative manner. Eviction or forced movement places huge stresses on Traveller education, as it may be difficult to make arrangements for the provision of education for children of an evicted family.

Other challenges facing Traveller parents include their own poor educational attainment and, for many, their negative experience in school, illiteracy, and the widespread experience of exclusion. Many Travellers attended special separate classes. Based on the 2002 census, almost two-thirds of the Travellers who gave the age at which their full-time education ceased left before the then statutory minimum age of fifteen. Many Traveller parents feel that they cannot take for granted things that settled parents generally do not even have to consider, for example that their child will be welcomed in some schools, will be treated fairly, and will have their needs dealt with in a respectful way. This can lead to ambivalence and a negative attitude on the part of some Traveller parents regarding the value of formal education.

An intensive, integrated and inter-agency response is needed if Traveller parents are to have confidence in the education system and if their children's rights are to be protected. For these parents the implementation of the recommendations in this report should bring about a situation where they become more confident that their concerns about formal education will be allayed. Some Traveller parents need assistance in enhancing their capacity to support their children in education. The wider Traveller community needs to support those Travellers who break the mould by staying in education beyond the usual years. Traveller parents need to be encouraged to return to education in accordance with section 6 (d) of the Education Act (1998):

to promote opportunities for adults, in particular adults who as children did not avail of or benefit from education in schools, to avail of educational opportunities through adult and continuing education.

4.4 Survey of Traveller Education Provision

The *Survey of Traveller Education Provision* conducted by the Department of Education and Science (published in May 2006) gathered the views of Traveller parents in eight different geographical settings. It found that parents expressed satisfaction with enrolment, inclusive practices and the involvement of their children in the extracurricular activities now evident in schools. The survey also reported that Traveller parents, based on their own lack of experience of education, have quite low educational expectations for their children and have little awareness of the opportunities that education can offer. However, most parents expressed unhappiness with progress in literacy and numeracy and with the cost of school uniforms (even with a Back-to-School clothing and footwear allowance) and other sundries. They were concerned about not understanding the post-primary system and about their children dropping out of post-primary education. Some Traveller parents felt that the education system is more suited to Traveller girls than boys and would like to see more practical subjects taught. They would like to see their children learning Irish. While acknowledging the achievement of the visiting teachers for Travellers, many of the principals and visiting teachers were of the view that the role of the visiting teacher required clarification.

4.5 Involvement of parents

Some Traveller parents are directly involved in education. An example of enabling parents to support their children is the involvement of Travellers as outreach workers in the School Completion Programme (SCP) in Clondalkin, Co. Dublin, as shown in example 1.

Example 1: Outreach workers in the Clondalkin School Completion Programme (SCP)
Two Traveller women are employed as outreach workers in the Clondalkin SCP. The outreach workers support Traveller parents in becoming more involved in their children's education, assist children and their parents in the transfer process from primary to post-primary, and liaise with the VTST, the SCP co-ordinator, the HSCL co-ordinator and the principals in schools. The outreach workers assist in the co-ordination of services between schools, families and others involved in the education of Traveller children.

There are also two Educational Equality Initiatives funded by the Department of Education and Science. One project, Parents and Traveller Education, is in Co. Mayo. It has two aims:

- that Traveller parents will understand the overall education system and be able to apply that understanding to the needs of their children by offering appropriate support

- that there will be greater mutual understanding and solidarity between Traveller parents and settled

parents in the general educational context, in particular in relation to representative structures.

The other project is the Traveller Homework Club and Parent Support in Ennis, Co. Clare. It also has two central objectives:

- to provide professional and voluntary support to children from the Traveller community in the area of homework support

- to provide development and training support to parents and volunteers that will enable them to participate and assist the tutors in the homework support club.

Taking another approach, access offices in higher education are developing initiatives to engage Traveller parents and their children in considering higher education as a viable option. An example is the DCU Access Service in Dublin City University, described in example 2.

Example 2: DCU Access Service
The DCU Access Service and the VTST in north Dublin have been collaborating in developing an initiative aimed at Travellers as part of the DCU Access Programme. Seminars for Traveller parents were organised in the university in 2004 and 2005, giving them, in the company of significant partners in education, the opportunity to engage in discussion, reflection and planning about their children's education. The process enables Traveller parents to engage in a real way, be empowered and be the main partners in developing an action plan that will support their children in progressing in education. Traveller children are also included in the mainstream access programme.

To be actively involved in education, parents, including Traveller parents, need information. The NCCA is preparing a DVD for parents on children's learning in primary schools. Pavee Point has also been involved in a project, Parents and Traveller Education, as shown in example 3.

Example 3: Pavee Point's Parents and Traveller Education
This project has two distinct objectives. One is to address the deficit of information and understanding among Traveller parents in relation to the education system and its structures. The second is to increase Traveller parents' involvement in school and parents' organisations. Pavee Point has consulted the National Parents' Council (NPC) as the project developed. The project:

- produced a video and DVD as a resource for training Traveller parents on the education system and their role in it

- disseminates the video and DVD among Traveller groups, VTST and NPC and others, and organise training workshops

- has established and organised a Traveller Parent Representative Forum

- will design a pilot scheme of regional training seminars to inform regional and national parents' councils of Traveller concerns

- will develop a good-practice booklet on Traveller inclusion, aimed at boards of management and parents' bodies.

It is hoped that more Traveller parents will become involved in education, both as workers and as volunteers. The primary health-care model of Traveller women's participation in the promotion of health is an initiative that the education system could learn from. The positive feature of the primary health-care model lies in the fact that Travellers themselves are trained to work with their own community on health issues.

4.6 Recommendations, proposed plans of action, and suggested time scale

General objective - Traveller Parents

Traveller parents should benefit from a comprehensive and inclusive programme of community-based education initiatives that will enable them to understand the education system, to participate in it, and to further support their children in education.

Traveller Parents Recommendations	Proposed plans of action	Suggested time scale
Recommendation 1 **Traveller parents' education:** Meet the educational needs of Traveller parents.	1. The Department of Education and Science, education providers and others should continue to: • heighten the awareness of existing educational provision by providing information, using DVD, face-to-face meetings, and outreach methods; existing resources are available for assisting in this area • enable Traveller parents to understand the long-term gains from engaging in lifelong learning, including further and higher education • encourage Traveller parents in gaining access to and engaging in further education courses that address their identified needs, including: • literacy • the Back-to-Education Initiative (BTEI) • the Vocational Training Opportunity Scheme (VTOS) • community education • post-Leaving Certificate courses.	Short
Recommendation 2 **Community development:** Build Traveller parents' understanding and value of education and their direct engagement with the system.	1. Provide information to Traveller parents so that they understand the education system, in particular pre-school, primary and post-primary and the role of the NEPS, NEWB, and others. The importance of continuous attendance and of not spending significant amounts of time out of school needs to be emphasised.	Short to medium
	2. Traveller parents should have high expectations of their children in school and be supported to encourage their children to a higher level of education than they may have had themselves. The VTST, HSCL scheme and SCP have an important continuing role in this area.	Medium
	3. A community development initiative aimed at Travellers as education workers should be considered. The introduction of such an initiative would require clarity between the role of the Traveller community education worker and that of the VTST and HSCL scheme. Such workers would require appropriate accredited training to give them the knowledge, skills and understanding required for such work.	Medium

Traveller Parents Recommendations	Proposed plans of action	Suggested time scale
	4. Traveller parents should be encouraged to become further involved in supports offered through the SCP, for example homework clubs, summer projects, mentoring schemes, and transfer programmes. Efforts should also be made to involve Traveller parents in the management structures of the SCP.	Short to medium
Recommendation 3 **Traveller representation:** Get Traveller parents involved in the representative structures.	1. Traveller parents should be encouraged to participate in representative structures. Those interested in becoming involved should be offered training, advice and support in that process.	Short to medium
Recommendation 4 **Parent-teacher communication:** Build effective communication between Traveller parents and teachers.	1. Colleges of education and providers of induction and continuing professional development (CPD) courses should ensure that the professional training of teachers addresses the need to maximise effective and respectful communication with parents from marginalised and minority backgrounds.	Short to medium
	2. Education centres should provide courses on equality and diversity, with a particular emphasis on intercultural education, anti-bias, anti-racism and anti-discrimination for teachers in their localities. Representatives of the Traveller community should be invited to become involved. Traveller organisations are already involved in the provision of training to statutory organisations.	Short to medium
	3. The Teaching Council should require the inclusion of compulsory modules on diversity and equality in the training of undergraduates and in the induction and CPD of teachers.	Short
	4. The Department of Education and Science should continue to support initiatives to build an effective dialogue between Traveller parents and teachers and the school community, between Traveller parents and the VTST, HSCL, and SCP, and between Traveller parents and higher education.	Short
Recommendation 5 **School-parent relationship:** Traveller parents should be included in all aspects of school life.	1. The Department of Education and Science should continue to take every opportunity to remind schools that they must take a whole-school approach to welcoming, acknowledging, respecting and having a positive attitude towards Traveller parents. In particular, Traveller parents should be invited and encouraged to take part in all aspects of school life in a manner similar to other parents. All parents, including Traveller parents, must be consulted about the educational needs of their children, and in particular where they require additional help. Such an inclusive approach must be reflected in the school plan and be an integral component in the whole-school evaluation process.	Short to medium

Traveller Parents Recommendations	Proposed plans of action	Suggested time scale
	2. Schools must have their enrolment and other policy documents available for Traveller parents in a format that is accessible. This should be verified as part of the whole-school evaluation (WSE) process.	Short
Recommendation 6 **An inter-agency approach:** This is required to respond effectively to Traveller parents' educational and other needs.	1. The Department of Environment, Heritage and Local Government's Traveller accommodation schemes should continue to give priority to the accommodation needs of Travellers.	Short to medium
	2. An intensive, integrated inter-agency response to Traveller parents' educational and other needs is required. This will involve co-ordination at the national level between the Department of Education and Science, Department of Social and Family Affairs, Department of Environment, Heritage and Local Government, Department of Enterprise, Trade and Employment, and Department of Health and Children. At the regional and local levels it will require co-ordination between DES regional offices, VTST, HSCL, SCP, NEWB, NEPS, VECs, all education providers and Travellers and their representative organisations to determine what is required to make education a viable and positive experience for Traveller parents and their children. The new DEIS Action Plan provides for the enhancement of integrated approaches and partnerships working to address educational disadvantage, in particular for three to eighteen-year-olds.	Short to medium

4.7 Expected outcome

The education system has to continue to evolve into an inclusive one that welcomes diversity in all its forms, including the Traveller community. In this regard, Traveller parents should:

• have a greater understanding of the value of education and of the education system

• participate in education, if they wish

• have high educational expectations for themselves

• continue to have high educational expectations for their children and encourage them to continue beyond compulsory education

• participate more fully in the education of their children.

Education providers should:

• engage actively with Traveller parents by including them as active partners in the education system.

Chapter 5
Pre-schools: Early-childhood education

5.1 Introduction

This chapter briefly examines the role of early-childhood education and in particular pre-schools for young Traveller children from the age of three up to school enrolment. It makes recommendations with proposed plans of action and time scales.

5.2 Early-childhood education

There is increasing recognition of the importance and value of the early years for all children's development. The *White Paper on Early Childhood Education: Ready to Learn* (1999) emphasises the importance of early-childhood education, particularly for disadvantaged children, and the need "to raise standards so that all Traveller children can receive early education of a high quality". There is also an increasing awareness that, in tackling educational disadvantage, prevention is better than cure. In other words, investment in the provision of early-childhood education, aimed at the most vulnerable, can reduce or avoid the necessity for spending on remedial measures later in the child's educational life, when they may not be as effective and may involve greater costs.

5.3 Traveller pre-schools

In mid-2005 there were forty-five special Traveller pre-schools. These were established largely through voluntary effort and later came to receive support from the Department of Education and Science, the Department of Health and Children, or voluntary and charitable organisations. Since 1992 the Department of Education and Science has provided annual in-service training for pre-school early-learning practitioners. Traveller children are also enrolled in some of the forty Early Start pre-schools that are funded by the Department of Education and Science.

5.4 Pre-Schools for Travellers: National Evaluation Report

Pre-Schools for Travellers: National Evaluation Report, published by the Evaluation Support and Research Unit (ESRU) of the Department of Education and Science in 2003, is based on an evaluation of Traveller pre-schools conducted by the Inspectorate in the school year 2000/01. The evaluation, conducted in twenty-three pre-schools, examined the management, accommodation and funding of the pre-schools, issues concerning staffing, the effectiveness of teaching and learning, and the ways in which parents and other partners were involved in the life of the pre-schools.

The report found that a range of agencies and volunteers manage these pre-schools and that staff members hold a wide variety of qualifications, ranging from little or no formal training to university degrees. The report noted that this diversity may be linked to a number of factors and that, given the origins of the pre-schools in the voluntary sector, it is likely that staff members in the pre-schools will continue to have a diverse range of qualifications for some time. However, it also recommends a greater provision of accredited courses, at both the pre-service and the in-service stage, so that early-learning practitioners and child-care assistants may acquire at least minimum qualifications over time.

5.5 Clarity on responsibility for Traveller pre-schools

Fundamentally, the ESRU evaluation points to the need for clarity in overall responsibility for the pre-schools. Many of the weaknesses in the Traveller pre-schools, such as the *ad hoc* nature of their management structures, the lack of curriculum and teaching guidelines, and the widely varying nature of the accommodation made available to them, may be attributed to the lack of a systematic and co-ordinated approach to the provision of pre-school services for Travellers.

5.6 Resource requirements

Many Traveller pre-schools are operating with inadequate resources and in unsuitable accommodation. The Department of Education and Science pays 98 per cent of teachers' salaries (early-learning practitioners) and transport costs for Traveller pre-schools. Further funding may be available from the Health Service Executive. However, many pre-schools are still struggling financially.

5.7 Plans towards the inclusive model

The existence of forty-five pre-schools exclusively for Traveller children means that Traveller and settled children living in the same geographical area miss an opportunity to interact with one another, go to pre-school together, and learn from one another. In DEIS (2005) the action plan will be aimed at early-childhood provision. The plan will aim to concentrate early-education action on those children, aged from three up to school enrolment age, who will subsequently attend the 180 urban primary schools participating in the SSP and serving the most disadvantaged communities, including the Traveller community. The extension of early-education support to areas served by other primary schools participating in the SSP will be considered at a later stage.

The future provision of an early-childhood education and care service for all young children, including young Traveller children, should be inclusive, well resourced, well managed, of high quality, with an appropriately trained staff, operating in suitable and good-quality premises. The plans for such educational provision for Traveller children should be regarded as an essential element of an integrated strategy for the provision of early-childhood education and care generally. The existing expertise and good practice built up in many of the pre-schools should not be lost but should be used to enhance integrated pre-school provision. Two Traveller pre-schools have already been integrated in mainstream pre-schools. Example 4 describes one such integrated play-school.

Example 4: St Catherine's Community Services Centre Play-School, Carlow

St Catherine's is an integrated play-school service for children from the local community, including the Traveller community and some non-Irish children. Such a mix enhances the children's experiences, and they get the opportunity from a very young age to embrace and learn about children from many cultures. Parents' involvement is actively encouraged. Activities are provided in a fun and interactive way. Intercultural activities include celebrating different festivals and telling stories about children living in different parts of the world and from different racial, national and minority groups. During circle time, differences are explored, such as likes and dislikes, different toys, forms of play, and music.

In the light of the Department of Education and Science's policy of inclusion, the NEOT, VTST and inspectors in the regional offices are actively exploring and facilitating the integration of segregated Traveller pre-schools with other quality early-years care and education services. Traveller families with resources should have access to privately run facilities on the same conditions as non-disadvantaged settled families.

5.8 OECD Thematic Review

The *OECD Thematic Review of Early Childhood Education and Care Policy in Ireland*, published in October 2004, calls for:

- the integration of all early-education and care policy and funding under one department or under a designated funding and policy agency

- the urgent formulation of a three-yearly National Plan for Early Childhood Services Development, with clearly spelt-out goals, targets, time-lines, responsibilities and accountability measures from co-operating departments.

While universal in intent, the plan should include annual targets and specific funding for important sub-systems, such as disadvantaged children, children from Traveller communities, and children with special needs.

5.9 Centre for Early Childhood Development and Education

The Centre for Early Childhood Development and Education was established in 2002. The centre's objectives include the development of a quality framework for early-childhood care and education and the development of targeted interventions for children who are educationally disadvantaged. With regard to Traveller children in pre-schools, the CECDE commissioned the Irish National Teachers' Organisation and Barnardo's to develop a continuing professional development programme for staff members and the management in pre-schools for Travellers. This involved six weekend training sessions for both staff members and the management of Traveller pre-schools. Example 5 lists some of the areas that were covered in the training sessions. The report of this one-year project is due in 2006.

Example 5: Training areas included in the INTO-Barnardo's programme

Play as an integral part of early-years education
Child profiling and curriculum planning
Parents as partners: encouraging their involvement
Diversity, ethos, and vision
Leadership and management skills
Management roles and responsibilities
Teamwork and communication

Source: Intouch, June 2005.

A draft of the quality framework for early-childhood care and education (referred to above) was produced in the autumn of 2005. Proposals for its publication and the testing and evaluation of the draft framework are both being considered by the Department of Education and Science.

5.10 National Council for Curriculum and Assessment

The NCCA is at present developing a national framework to support all children's early learning. To inform the process, in 2004 the NCCA published

Towards a Framework for Early Learning, a discussion paper that makes specific reference to Traveller education. The purpose of the framework is to help ensure that all children have appropriately enriching, challenging and enjoyable learning opportunities throughout their early-childhood years. In May 2005 the NCCA published *Towards a Framework for Early Learning: Final Consultation Report.*

The NCCA's framework for early learning and the CECDE's quality framework will both greatly increase the potential to embed quality early-learning experiences for all children and particularly for those in early-childhood education and care. The two frameworks are being developed in close collaboration.

5.11 Government Committee on Children

A High-Level Working Group on Early Childhood Education and Care was set up by the Government Committee on Children to make recommendations on an integrated national policy for child care and early education. The policy is to result in improved co-ordination at the national and the local level and to incorporate a child-centred approach to the provision of services. The National Children's Office is chairing this group.

5.12 Training in equality and diversity

Training in equality and diversity in early-childhood education and care is the key to successful integration and inclusion. Such training has been provided through the Pavee Point "Éist" initiatives in Co. Mayo and Dublin, as described in example 6.

Example 6: "Éist"
Pavee Point published Éist in 2001. Éist provides a diversity approach to training for policy-makers, trainers and practitioners involved in early-years education, care, and training. It was published in response to the growing needs of educators and children living in an increasingly multicultural and intercultural society. Diversity education will benefit and enhance the lives of children attending early-years services, as it equally acknowledges, respects and values all children and enables them to learn to respect and positively value each other's differences and similarities. In 2004 Pavee Point published Ar an mBealach, which acts as a support in providing diversity and equality training. This manual discusses issues of racism and discrimination in early-childhood education, care, and training. A range of Traveller jigsaws was also produced.

5.13 Opportunities for Traveller employment

The provision of early-childhood education is an area with high potential for the employment of Travellers. Already a number of Travellers are employed as service-providers, early-learning practitioners, and assistants. Their employment provides positive role models for all the children and parents, both Traveller and settled. It also means that Travellers bring their expertise on Traveller issues to the planning and provision of the service.

5.14 Recommendations, proposed plans of action, and suggested time scale

General objective - Early-childhood education

Traveller children should have access to an inclusive, well-resourced, well-managed, high-quality early-childhood education, with an appropriately trained staff operating in good-quality premises.

Early childhood education Recommendations	Proposed plans of action	Suggested time scale
Recommendation 1 **Structures:** Create a mechanism in the Department of Education and Science for administering the provision of pre-school and early-childhood education.	1. Responsibility should be taken within the Department of Education and Science for providing for the future development and integration of all aspects of early-childhood education, including Traveller pre-schools. Plans should be established for achieving this, starting with the establishment of a properly staffed Early Years Development Unit (EYDU) within the Department, as called for by the OECD Thematic Review (2004).	Short term
	2. Significant investment is required in the area of early-childhood education.	Short term
	3. As recommended by the ESRU report, a common funding arrangement should be established for all pre-schools, and this should cover all costs, including the cost of child-care assistants. The DES should, as an immediate step, increase the 98 per cent grant for teachers' salaries to 100 per cent and bring the equipment grant into line with equipment grants allocated to Early Start centres.	Short term
	4. Recommendations on Traveller pre-schools, as described in the ESRU National Evaluation Report, should be implemented.	Short term
	5. Clarity on overall responsibility for pre-schools should be provided.	Short term
	6. The work of the High-Level Working Group on Early Childhood Education and Care should provide clarity on responsibilities and on co-ordination of the provision of early-childhood education and care services.	Short term
	7. As an interim measure, where necessary and appropriate, the department should support the management agencies of existing pre-schools.	Short term
Recommendation 2 **Inclusion:** Change the grounds on which pre-school education to Travellers is provided to an inclusive, integrated service.	1. A mapping exercise should be undertaken to provide data for a phased implementation plan for amalgamating existing Traveller-only pre-school provision with existing and future early-childhood education services, including Early Start and DEIS early education provision. (See recommendation 3.) Within five years, half the existing pre-schools should be amalgamated.	Short term

Early childhood education Recommendations	Proposed plans of action	Suggested time scale
	2. In implementing the policy of inclusion, all support services should be provided in a way that is based on identified need rather than on Traveller identity.	Medium term
Recommendation 3 **Availability and take-up:** Increase the availability and take-up by Traveller children of pre-school education.	1. A continuous projection of the number and location of pre-school places required for all children from disadvantaged areas, including Traveller children.	Short term
	2. The availability of pre-schools should be increased, even beyond the proposed 180 DEIS sites. Provision should be developed to meet the projected need in places accessible to both communities.	Medium term
	3. Mechanisms should be established for increasing take up in early-childhood education by Travellers and in particular by those who are nomadic.	Short term
	4. All pre-schools should have enrolment policies that guard against discrimination, bias, and racism.	Short term
Recommendation 4 **Quality education:** Improve the quality of education available in pre-schools.	1. All early-childhood staff members in state-funded schemes should be appropriately trained, made aware of best practice, and be skilled in dealing positively with diversity. A budget for such initiatives should be available. The CECDE quality framework should inform quality standards.	Short to medium term
	2. CPD of early-learning practitioners and child-care workers should be given priority and made more comprehensive.	Short to medium term
	3. Mainstream the intercultural approach in all pre-service training and CPD of early-childhood education staff.	Short to medium term
	4. Develop intercultural materials and resources for use in early-childhood education services as part of the NCCA's Framework for Early Learning. Such materials should be developed in consultation with Traveller child-care workers and with Traveller children.	Short to medium term
	5. The provision of existing and future early-childhood education should be continuously evaluated and monitored by the Inspectorate of the Department of Education and Science.	Short to medium term
Recommendation 5 **Equality:** Increase the emphasis on equality in the planning and provision of early-childhood education services, and eliminate the potential for discrimination and racism.	1. Management committees of state-funded pre-schools should establish equality-proofing mechanisms; in particular, they should have active, inclusive, equality-proofed policies on admission, which should be implemented and regularly reviewed.	Short to medium term

Early childhood education Recommendations	Proposed plans of action	Suggested time scale
Recommendation 6 **Recruitment of Travellers:** Increase the number of Travellers who are employed in the provision of early-childhood education services in a sustained and active manner.	1. Identify and implement positive action measures, in a sustained and active manner, to increase access to staff training for Travellers for all roles in the early-childhood education system.	Short to medium term
Recommendation 7 **Location and future development:** No new segregated Traveller pre-schools should be established.	1. Pre-schools for Travellers should not be established on halting sites or on other Traveller-specific sites. 2. No new segregated Traveller pre-schools should be established. Traveller children should be catered for through general pre-school provision.	Short to medium term Short to Medium term

5.15 Expected outcome

Within the five-year span,

- half the segregated pre-schools for Travellers should be integrated, and all should be integrated within ten years, where possible

- Traveller children should have access to an inclusive, well-resourced, well-managed, high-quality, publicly funded early-childhood education, with an appropriately trained staff (including representatives of the Traveller community), operating in quality premises

- the CECDE Quality Framework and the NCCA's Framework for Early Learning should have been approved and implemented and should be the quality standard or mark in all pre-schools and other early-learning settings.

Chapter 6
Primary education

6.1 Introduction

This chapter outlines the provision made for Traveller pupils within primary education. It summarises the measures taken by the Department of Education and Science to promote the primary education of Traveller pupils, identifies educational issues, makes recommendations, and proposes plans of action with time scales.

6.2 Statistics

In 2003/04 there were 3,278 primary schools in the Republic, with an enrolment of 446,000 children between the ages of four and thirteen. Approximately 26,000 primary teachers are employed in these schools. In 2004/05 it was estimated that almost 6,000 Traveller children were enrolled in primary schools, which equates to virtually 100 per cent enrolment. The exact number of Traveller children in primary schools is not known, because that specific figure is not formally sought from schools. No data is collected on ethnicity or other minority identity.

6.3 Measures by the Department of Education and Science

Traveller children are entitled to all the services available to settled children. Additional measures taken by the Department of Education and Science to promote the primary education of Traveller children in recent years include the following:

1. the adoption of inclusion as a central policy, with all special classes for Traveller children in primary schools having been phased out by the end of the school year 2003/04 and only one special primary school for Travellers remaining after June 2005

2. ensuring that the department's policy of age-appropriate placement is applied to all children in primary schools, including Traveller children

3. the provision of a National Education Officer for Travellers to promote the department's policy in primary schools

4. the appointment of resource teachers for Travellers to provide specific educational support for Traveller children

5. a national Visiting Teacher Service for Traveller Education, the Home-School-Community Liaison scheme, and the School Completion Programme, all

of which include the needs of Traveller children within their remit

6. the provision of continuing professional development courses for principals, teachers and Traveller parents by the NEOT and the VTST, in collaboration with the Inspectorate and education centres

7. an enhanced capitation grant in respect of Traveller pupils enrolled in primary schools (where an RTT has been appointed) of €296 for pupils under the age of twelve and €495 for pupils over twelve; this compares with the standard capitation grant of €141

8. mainstream transport for Traveller children to get to and from primary school and, in certain circumstances, the provision of special transport, with the Department of Education and Science paying 98 per cent of the running costs of approved special transport schemes

9. the publication of *Guidelines on Traveller Education in Primary Schools* (2002) and *Guidelines on Intercultural Education in the Primary School* (2005)

10. including the needs of Traveller children in school development planning

11. the publication of an information booklet for schools on the Equal Status Acts in 2005

12. the publication of *Delivering Equality of Opportunity in Schools: An Action Plan for Educational Inclusion* in May 2005, and its implementation.

6.4 Allocation of teachers

Under the disadvantaged initiatives for primary schools, the Department of Education and Science operates a policy whereby it excludes from the valid enrolment all pupils for whom an additional teaching resource has already been provided (RTTs in the case of Traveller children and special-needs class teachers in the case of children with special educational needs) for the purposes of calculating staffing to implement reduced pupil-teacher ratios.

Recommendation 6 at the end of this chapter puts forward a possible future scenario for RTTs that takes a phased approach. In the initial phase it is recommended that an audit of existing RTTs be carried out. Following the audit, it suggests in the context of inclusion and integration that Traveller pupils be counted in the general enrolment, and that Travellers also be included in the general allocation for special educational needs. It is recommended that no additional resources be allocated on the grounds of membership of the Traveller community but only on the grounds of identified educational need. Based on the audit findings, the RTTs would be assigned to the general enrolment allocation and also to the general allocation for special educational needs, while the remainder would provide pastoral care, learning support and home-school links and be involved in team teaching. The term "resource teacher for Travellers" should be replaced with a more generic term, such as "learning-support teacher". Such a policy would ensure that all pupils, including Traveller pupils, would benefit from the services of these teachers, who have developed specialist expertise.

It is recommended that these proposals be reviewed in the fourth year of the strategy being implemented, and that recommendations for future provision evolve from this fourth-year review. Therefore, based on the audit findings, there would be no diminution of teaching resources for schools that have Traveller pupils on their roll. Instead this resource would be available to all pupils, including Traveller pupils.

6.5 Identified educational issues

The participation by Traveller children at the primary level has improved greatly in recent years. The findings of the *Survey of Traveller Education Provision* (STEP) carried out by the Inspectorate, published in May 2006, notes that the main outstanding issues to be addressed relate to:

- **Attendance.** The attendance of Traveller children at the primary level is an issue of deep concern. The STEP found that the average attendance rate by Traveller children is approximately 80 per cent. This average, as noted in the survey, includes figures varying from 35 per cent to 100 per cent, being lowest for those who lived in unofficial halting sites.

- **Attainment.** The results that emerged from a data analysis of standardised test results for Traveller pupils carried out for the STEP survey suggest that more than 60 per cent of Traveller pupils are below the 20th percentile in English reading and in mathematics, while 2 per cent are in the top (80-100) quintile.

The implementation of recommendations and plans of action for addressing these two core issues through school attendance policies and through an emphasis on improving individual levels of Traveller pupils' attainment will be of critical importance to the success of future Traveller education.

In addition to the problems described above, concerns were expressed in the submissions received as part of the consultation process that many Traveller children do not obtain access to the full primary school curriculum. Schools should be sensitive to the fact that children, if they have to be withdrawn from class for learning support, should not have any particular area of the curriculum neglected. Team-teaching approaches, which are a feature of the work of a number of schools at present, need to be further developed to ensure that children have access to the full curriculum. Only those Traveller children with identified educational needs should receive learning support.

The enrolment of Traveller pupils is not reflected in the school population of many communities. Many principals who are willing to enrol Traveller pupils note that others in their area do not enrol Traveller pupils and yet can expand, gain extra buildings, and enrol settled pupils from the school willing to enrol Traveller pupils.

The education of the more nomadic Traveller children presents a specific challenge to local schools, to nomadic parents, and to the Department of Education and Science. At present, many schools have difficulties in meeting the needs of the nomadic children who enrol for short periods throughout the year. (See section 10.3 for further information.)

Many Traveller children experience difficulties in getting homework done regularly. For some this may be because of their poor home accommodation; for others it may be because their parents have not got a strong educational background. While some support structures have been established for dealing with this issue, there is nevertheless a great need to expand these structures.

Difficulties exist in respect of the psychological assessment of Traveller children. Initiatives taken by the NEPS and the VTST may need to be further developed. An awareness of Traveller children's needs is necessary, together with appropriate assessment and test instruments, free from cultural bias.

6.6 Consultations with Traveller learners and parents, 2004

The findings from the survey of Traveller parents and learners conducted by Traveller organisations as part of the development process for this report drew attention to a number of areas, including the following:

- **Enrolment.** Difficulties are still being encountered by some Traveller parents in enrolling their children in certain primary schools, despite the fact that section

21 (2) of the Education Act (1998) requires that "the school plan shall state the objectives of the school relating to equality of access to, and participation in, the school and the measures which the school proposes to take to achieve those objectives..." and section 29 (c) provides an appeal process for dealing with issues relating to refusal to "enrol a student in a school."

- **Negative experiences.** While many Travellers have had positive experiences with schools, it was found in this consultation process that the majority of experiences were negative. Traveller children are constantly aware that their identity may pose a problem for them in school, whether in their relations with teachers or among their settled peers. Lack of validation of identity often reinforces Traveller children's inclination to hide their identity in order to fit in and also to avoid discrimination, bullying, or harassment.

- **Parental concerns.** Some Traveller parents expressed deep concern about the low attainment of their children, particularly in relation to literacy and numeracy. Some parents find it difficult to visit the local primary school and to communicate with the principal or teachers in the school. They find it daunting to visit the local school to seek enrolment forms or to ask for information about the school and its curriculum. This could, in part, be due to their own negative experiences of education, their poor literacy level, or experiences of hostility from the settled community. Many schools may not be aware of the difficulties that Traveller parents have in this regard, and it was noted that many teachers may not know how to deal with complex issues relating to Traveller identity or to incidents of bullying, discrimination, and discipline.

- **Consideration of the Traveller viewpoint.** In some schools the curricular provision and policies being formulated (such as those regarding enrolment, bullying, and harassment) do not give due consideration to the impact they may have on Traveller parents and their children and on their relations with the wider school community.

6.7 Reading Literacy in Disadvantaged Primary Schools Survey, 2004

This survey by the Educational Research Centre showed that Traveller pupils:

achieved significantly lower mean scores than their counterparts from the settled community (up to almost

one full standard deviation). Mean score estimates for pupils who are Travellers range from 85.9 in sixth class to 88.0 in first class, compared with approximately 100.0 for pupils from the settled community.

Table 5: Mean achievement scores for members of the Traveller and settled communities, by school class

	First class	Third class	Sixth class
Travellers	88.0	87.7	85.9
Settled community	100.5	100.4	100.2

Source: ERC report, 2004, table 5.7.

There are schools that successfully integrate Travellers, as example 7 demonstrates.

Example 7: Inclusion of Traveller children in mainstream education
The staff felt that it may not be appropriate to overtly identify Travellers for the purpose of withdrawal and learning support. This could lead to discrimination and alienation. This is the last thing you want.

So all the resources were grouped together: RTTs and Learning Support Teachers (LSTs). LSTs and RTTS now had a mixture of mainstream and Traveller pupils. All the time, we ensured that Travellers were benefiting from the resources that had been allocated to the school for them by the DES, but this benefit was applied in an integrated way.

Needless to say, parental permission was sought at all times to have Travellers avail of this support. Credit must go to the staff for their willingness to become involved in this integration process and for making it successful...

Our Traveller pupils participate in all school activities, and some have represented the school in hurling, camogie, soccer, and athletics...

Parents are quite comfortable in coming to the school - they are anxious that their child does as well as possible academically. As a parent said to me lately, "Do whatever is best for my child". This shows that we are trusted to do that.

The Traveller families have been and are involved in programmes run by our Home-School-Community Liaison Co-ordinator. This is further evidence of inclusiveness.

Source: John Devitt, *The Inclusive School* (2004), p. 68-69. John Devitt is principal of Sacred Heart Primary School, Roscrea, Co. Tipperary.

The Tullamore Travellers' Movement after-school programme is another example of integration, as example 8 shows.

Example 8: Tullamore Travellers' Movement after-school programme
This after-school programme is an integrated project that caters for children in second class to fifth class. It welcomes children from all backgrounds and embraces diversity. At present the programme consists of 60 per cent Traveller children and 40 per cent settled children. The children are encouraged to develop their educational, social, emotional and physical skills with the guidance of a team of skilled and personally committed workers. While homework assistance is available, there is equal emphasis on such activities as arts and crafts, sports, and trips. Through consultation with teachers, parents, and the children, the programme is based on the children's needs.

6.8 Recommendations, proposed plans of action, and suggested time scale

General objective - Primary education

Traveller children should have equality of access, equality of participation and equality of outcome in a fully inclusive primary education system that respects Traveller identity and culture.

Primary Education Recommendations	Proposed plans of action	Suggested time scale
Recommendation 1 **Inclusion:** End all segregated provision at the primary level.	1. The Department of Education and Science should manage the phasing out, over an appropriate period, of the remaining Traveller-only primary school.	Short term
Recommendation 2 **Enrolment:** Make the inclusion of Travellers an explicit part of the school plan and also of enrolment and other policies.	1. All primary schools, in compliance with the Education Act (1998), should have a school plan that sets out their objectives relating to equality of access. Their enrolment and other policy documents in such areas as supervision, bullying, homework, outings, consultation with parents and home-school liaison should welcome Travellers, celebrate diversity, acknowledge Traveller nomadism, promote interculturalism, and be sensitive to the needs of Traveller parents and pupils. The school plan and policy documents should be ratified by the board of management and should be made available to all parents. Their implementation should be regularly reviewed and amended as considered necessary. 2. During whole-school evaluations (WSE), school plans, enrolment and other policies, with particular reference to Traveller education and the particular needs of nomadic Travellers, should be formally evaluated. The enrolment of Traveller pupils should happen in all school communities and not be concentrated in one or two schools. This should be monitored by WSE. The VTST should continue to work towards facilitating the parents' choice in school placement and in informing them of the provisions of section 29 of the Education Act (1998) if they need to use the appeal system.	
Recommendation 3 **Attendance:** Develop the education welfare service and other home-school support to achieve as near full attendance as possible.	1. The services provided by the NEWB should be further developed to support schools in establishing effective attendance strategies for all pupils, including Travellers, that are culturally sensitive. To maximise attendance, Traveller parents should be involved in a co-ordinated and co-operative process with the VTST, RTTs, education welfare officers, HSCL co-ordinators, SCP co-ordinators, other staff members in the school, CWOs, and youth workers. To achieve maximum attendance, the rights and responsibilities of all concerned, in particular Traveller parents, who have the primary responsibility in this regard, need to be clearly set out.	Short to medium term

Primary Education Recommendations	Proposed plans of action	Suggested time scale
	2. The recommendations in the STEP survey need to be analysed to determine how attendance levels can be improved. By the end of the five-year life of the proposed strategy the target should be that all Traveller pupils have absences of less than twenty days per year. This target needs to be monitored. Recognition must be given to those Traveller pupils who attend regularly.	Short to medium term
Recommendation 4 **Attainment:** Raise the attainment level of Traveller children to be on a par with national standards.	1. The recommendations in the STEP report (2006) and in *Literacy and Numeracy in Disadvantaged Schools* (2005) should be considered to determine how attainment levels can be improved.	Short to medium term
	2. All pupils, including Travellers, should have access to the full curriculum and should be encouraged to achieve to their highest capabilities.	Short term
	3. Learning support in primary schools should be implemented in accordance with the principles and methods described in Learning Support Guidelines (2000). An integrated, collaborative and in-class learning support system should be adopted, where appropriate, in all primary schools for all children, including Travellers, who have identified educational needs. The parents of children receiving learning support need to be consulted and informed about what is involved and the benefits to be gained, and they should be regularly brought up to date. This should be evaluated in the WSE.	Short to medium term
	4. Individual learning plans should be drawn up in respect of every child, including Traveller children, availing of special educational needs support, and their parents should be consulted in accordance with departmental policy.	Short to medium term
	5. The department's Learning Support Guidelines should provide guidance to schools in relation to the critical area of attainment (with particular reference to literacy and numeracy) by Traveller children with identified learning difficulties. Other issues in this area that need to be addressed include: • the CPD of teachers to address and improve pupil attainment • regular monitoring of attainment at individual pupil level, sensitive to Traveller culture • systematic planning at individual level to meet identified needs	Short to medium term

Primary Education Recommendations	Proposed plans of action	Suggested time scale
	• planning in respect of the needs of nomadic pupils	
	• establishing appropriate targets, outcomes and time scales for improvement in attainment for each pupil.	
	6. Total levels of progress accruing from the investment in extra educational supports for Traveller children should be regularly monitored at the national level by the DES.	Medium term
	7. Appropriate instruments (free from cultural bias etc.) should be designed (such as positive profiles that concentrate on what the pupil can do) and made available to NEPS psychologists for the diagnostic and screening assessment of all children, including Travellers. Parents should be kept informed, using appropriate media.	Medium term
	8. Schools should continue to adopt an inclusive whole-school approach to responding to the educational needs of all pupils, including Traveller pupils. This will involve systematic planning by the school team, taking a partnership approach (principal, class teachers, and all categories of learning-support teachers, as well as VTST, HSCL, SCP, etc.). Work by each member of the team should complement and reinforce that of other members. Systematic planning by the school team should take place at the individual pupil level through establishing targets and tracking systems and by regularly monitoring progress, with the aim of supporting pupils in achieving their full educational potential.	Medium term
Recommendation 5 **Training:** Equality and diversity training should be a compulsory component of the pre-service, induction and continuing professional development (CPD) of teachers. It should continue to be a component of the CPD of inspectors and of the personnel of the School Development Planning Initiative (SDPI) and Primary Curriculum Support Programme (PCSP).	1. The Teaching Council should require the inclusion of compulsory modules on equality and diversity in initial teacher training courses. It should also recommend the inclusion of diversity and equality in induction training courses and in CPD courses for teachers in conjunction with the relevant experts.	Short term
	2. Following the publication of *Guidelines on Traveller Education in Primary Schools* (2002) and the *NCCA's Intercultural Guidelines for Primary Schools* (2005) it is vital that the Department of Education and Science provide funding for continuing training in equality and diversity, to include interculturalism, anti-bias, anti-racism, and anti-discrimination, for the induction and CPD of boards of management, patrons, trustees, teachers and principals and to facilitate the continuing development of an intercultural, inclusive school that deals positively with diversity from a whole-school standpoint. The Inspectorate, SDPI and PCSP should continue to include equality and diversity in their training courses.	Short to medium term

Primary Education Recommendations	Proposed plans of action	Suggested time scale
	3. Modules on different cultures, including Traveller culture, should form a distinct and core part of all equality and diversity training.	Short to medium term
Recommendation 6 **Resource teachers for Travellers:** Short-term and medium-term recommendations are made on the grounds that educational needs rather than Traveller identity should be a trigger for additional resources.	In the short term, an audit of existing RTT posts is required. Following the audit, and based on its findings, 1. For schools participating in disadvantaged initiatives: • Travellers should be included in the valid enrolment for the purposes of allocating additional staffing to implement reduced class sizes • Travellers should be included in the valid enrolment for the purposes of allocating special-teaching resources under the new general allocation system, September 2005 (see section 10.4.3) • RTT posts should be used by schools to implement these decisions and for the betterment of all pupils • schools should be allowed to retain the remaining RTT post (or posts) pending the findings of the review in year 4, as outlined below, to provide learning support and to be involved in team teaching, home-school links, and pastoral support • a team approach should be implemented in assisting children with identified educational needs • parents must be consulted and their agreement obtained regarding additional learning support for their children. Pending the review in year 4 there should be no diminution of teaching resources for schools with Traveller children with identified educational needs on the roll as a result of these recommendations. 2. For schools not included in disadvantaged initiatives: • Travellers should be included in the valid enrolment for the purposes of allocating special teaching resources under the general allocation system • the RTT posts should be used by schools to implement this policy • schools should retain the remaining RTT post (or posts), pending the findings of the review in year 4, to provide learning support and to be involved in team teaching, home-school links, and pastoral support	Short term Short to medium term Medium term

Primary Education Recommendations	Proposed plans of action	Suggested time scale
	• a team approach should be implemented in assisting children with identified educational needs	
	• parents must be consulted and their agreement obtained regarding additional learning support for their children.	
	Pending the review in year 4 there should be no diminution of teaching resources for schools with Traveller children with identified educational needs on the roll as a result of these recommendations	
	The implementation of these new measures should be reviewed after four years. Consideration in such a review should be given, among other things, to the following questions:	
	• Within this interim period, are the needs of all children, but in particular Traveller children, being met?	
	• Is phasing out the category of "resource teacher for Travellers" and incorporating the additional resources in mainstream provision an appropriate model?	
	• Has the inclusion of Travellers in the valid enrolment for the purposes of calculating staffing to implement reduced pupil-teacher ratios been of benefit to the Traveller pupils and to all pupils?	
	• Has the inclusion of Travellers in the general allocation system for special educational needs worked?	
	A circular outlining any new arrangements should be issued to schools.	
Recommendation 7 **Visiting Teacher Service for Travellers:** Review, evaluate and adapt the service, if necessary.	1. The VTST should be reviewed in the light of the introduction of new management structures in 2005, the establishment of the NEWB in 2002, the HSCL scheme, the publication of *Delivering Equality of Opportunity in Schools: An Action Plan for Educational Inclusion* (2005), acknowledging the fact that an estimated 40 per cent of Traveller pupils will be enrolled in schools not eligible for availing of DEIS initiatives.	Short to medium term
Recommendation 8 **Traveller parents:** Parents should be encouraged and supported to take an active part in all aspects of school life.	1. The Department of Education and Science, in consultation with the National Parents' Council, Traveller NGOs and representatives of Traveller parents should encourage initiatives that support Traveller parents in taking an active part in all aspects of school life.	Short to medium term

Primary Education Recommendations	Proposed plans of action	Suggested time scale
	2. Boards of management should ensure that Traveller parents are included in all aspects of their work and should establish measures to ensure that Traveller parents have access to their children's school, should understand the aims and objectives of the school, and should meet the principal or all their teachers and talk about, for example, extracurricular activities, the educational progress of their children and other issues as the need arises. Such access should continue to be facilitated by the VTST and the HSCL co-ordinators.	Medium term
	3. All education partners should ensure that Traveller parents have access to information about the education system.	Short to medium term
	4. Traveller organisations should continue to support Traveller parents and encourage them to take an active part in all aspects of school life.	Short to medium term
Recommendation 9 **School development planning:** School planning and the School Development Planning Initiative (SDPI) should have an increased emphasis on equality, on inclusion, and on the educational needs of Travellers.	1. Through the SDPI, schools should recognise, accept and support all Travellers in relation to the education of their children. This should be reflected in their school development plans.	Short term
	2. Equality targets and progress indicators should be included in the school development planning process.	Short to medium term
Recommendation 10 **Funding:** The provision of additional funding specifically for Travellers should be reviewed.	1. The system of providing additional capitation grants on the grounds of identity should be replaced, in a carefully planned manner and over an appropriate period, with a system that is based on identified educational needs. In the meantime a review should be undertaken of how schools are spending the enhanced grant now being made available to support the education of Traveller children, with recommendations being made on the most appropriate arrangements to be applied for the future.	Medium term
	2. The special additional capitation funding provided for Traveller children over the age of twelve in primary schools should cease.	Short term
Recommendation 11 **Transport:** School transport should be provided on the same conditions as for settled pupils.	1. Traveller children should use the mainstream school transport scheme in operation at present. Only in exceptional circumstances, based on special needs, should special transport be provided as a positive action measure.	Short to Medium term

Primary Education Recommendations	Proposed plans of action	Suggested time scale
Recommendation 12 **Evaluation:** Evaluate and monitor provision for Travellers in the primary system through the whole-school evaluation process.	1. The WSE, as part of its formal remit, should evaluate provision for Traveller pupils, including nomadic pupils, where they are enrolled in a school and should determine whether the school has equality and diversity policies that are being implemented.	Short to Medium term
Recommendation 13 **Traveller community education workers:** Consider establishing a network of Traveller community education workers.	1. The development of community initiatives aimed at Travellers as education workers should be considered. Such workers would require appropriate accredited training to give them the knowledge, skills and understanding required for the work. The introduction of such an initiative would require clarity about their role vis-à-vis the VTST, HSCL, and others. Such initiatives should be pursued in a co-ordinated manner with other relevant state agencies.	Medium term
Recommendation 14 **Other issues:** Nomadism, culture, data collection, access to homework clubs, consultation with pupils and access to higher education all need to be addressed.	1. Nomadism, how it affects primary schools and the ways to address the needs of nomadic Traveller pupils should be examined and recommendations made. (See section 10.3.)	Short to medium term
	2. If a number of children, including Traveller children, with identified educational needs arrive in a school after October, a temporary appointment should be made in the school to provide immediate assistance to the children. The number of children needed to qualify for additional assistance would depend on the particular circumstances of the school. Parental consent for such provision should be sought.	Short term
	3. Traveller culture should be an integral part of the intercultural curriculum and be represented positively in each school.	Short to medium term
	4. Data on pupils in primary schools, including Traveller pupils, needs to be collected to ensure that targets can be set, progress monitored, and outcome evaluated.	Short to medium term
	5. Traveller pupils, like other pupils, should continue to have access to homework clubs.	Short to medium term
	6. A random sample of pupils, including Traveller pupils, should be consulted every two years to find out what they think about primary education, to listen to their recommendations, and to give them a voice to present their views.	Short to medium term
	7. The encouragement of young people to aspire to higher education should start in fifth and sixth class in primary school. Young Traveller children should be encouraged to consider a career within the education system.	Medium term

6.9 Expected outcome

All Traveller children attending primary school should
have equality of access, participation and outcome in
a school that is fully inclusive. Schools should:

• have high expectations for the educational outcome
  for Traveller children

• provide information to Traveller parents on life in
  their school, using media that are accessible; Traveller
  parents should be encouraged to take an active
  part in all aspects of school life

• continue to provide all children, including Traveller
  children, who have identified educational needs with
  additional learning support in an integrated setting

• adopt a team approach to improving attendance by
  setting targets and monitoring progress.

Chapter 7
Post-primary education

7.1 Introduction

This chapter outlines the provision for Traveller pupils within post-primary education. It summarises the measures taken by the Department of Education and Science to promote the post-primary education of Traveller pupils, identifies educational issues, makes recommendations, and proposes plans of action with time scales.

7.2 Statistics

In 2003/04 there were 743 post-primary schools in the Republic, with 337,851 pupils attending. It is estimated that 85 per cent of Traveller children transfer to post-primary school. For the school year 2004/05 approximately 1,850 Traveller pupils, out of a total of 4,000 Travellers aged between thirteen and eighteen (inclusive), were enrolled in post-primary schools.

7.3 Measures by the Department of Education and Science

The measures taken by the Department of Education and Science to promote the post-primary education of Traveller pupils in recent years have included the following:

1. the provision of a National Education Officer for Travellers to promote the participation of Travellers in post-primary education and to promote department policy

2. the allocation of ex-quota teaching hours in accordance with the number of Travellers enrolled in post-primary schools.

    There are approximately 140 whole-time-equivalent posts that provide specific educational support and pastoral care for Traveller pupils attending post-primary schools. Circular 43/99 describes the support available for post-primary schools enrolling Traveller pupils.

3. a national VTST for Traveller education, the HSCL scheme, and the SCP, which include the needs of Traveller children within their remit

4. the provision of continuing professional development to principals and teachers by the NEOT and VTST

5. a supplementary-level capitation grant of €427 for each Traveller pupil enrolled in a post-primary school, in addition to the standard capitation of €298

6. the provision of mainstream transport for Traveller pupils and in certain circumstances the provision of special transport

7. the publication of *Guidelines on Traveller Education in Second Level Schools* (2002) and an information booklet for schools on the Equal Status Acts, 2005

8. the preparation of *Guidelines on Intercultural Education in the Post-Primary School*, being prepared by the NCCA for issue to schools in 2006

9. the establishment of after-school and holiday-time support.

    For example, the SCP is aimed at individual young people of school-going age who are at risk, both in and out of school, and arranges supports for dealing with inequalities in education access, participation, and outcome. In 2004/05 approximately 1,300 Traveller children were identified by this initiative in primary and post-primary schools.

10. the publication of *Delivering Equality of Opportunity in Schools: An Action Plan for Educational Inclusion* (2005).

7.4 Identified educational issues

7.4.1 Successful transfer from primary to post-primary school

Progression from primary to post-primary school is recognised by most schools as a crucial transition in the educational continuum. Pupils who fail to successfully make this transition are more at risk of potential early school-leaving or educational under-achievement. A study by the Economic and Social Research Institute on behalf of the NCCA, *Moving Up: The Experiences of First-Year Students in Post-Primary Schools* (2004), examined this issue in detail and emphasised its particular importance for groups of pupils at risk. The study noted that "students from non-national or Traveller backgrounds report more transition difficulties than other students". It provides a number of suggestions for successful transfer, including the creation of a comprehensive integration "package" presented in a positive, informal climate. Such a package could include open days, greater pre-entry contact with the pupils and their parents, post-primary personnel visiting feeder primary schools, an induction day, liaison between primary and post-primary schools on the transfer of relevant educational information, an information module for sixth-class pupils that would provide information on post-primary schools, the involvement in extracurricular activities and pastoral care of first-year class tutors or year head involved with helping pupils to settle in, and a pupil mentoring system.

Many of these initiatives are already found as part of the successful transfer programme in post-primary schools. The need to continue to develop effective measures for ensuring successful transition from primary to post-primary is an important element of the department's DEIS Action Plan and is one of the most important challenges to be addressed. It involves the whole-school community if the successful transfer of young people is to become a reality.

There are many examples of good practice in this transition from primary to post-primary school, and one of these is described briefly in example 9.

Example 9: Example of a transfer programme
Deis na Gaillimhe Consortium, led by Galway City VEC, developed a post-primary transition programme called "OK! Let's go". The programme addresses the problems and fears of young people associated with the transition from primary to post-primary school, particularly those who are potential early school-leavers. The programme takes a three-pronged approach:

- In primary school a whole-class approach and a targeted group approach is taken.

- In the transition year, summer activities are organised by youth and community groups.

- In post-primary there are induction and monitoring procedures for the first month in the new school, and there are also a number of follow-up actions that identify potential early school-leavers.

7.4.2 Enrolment policies
The operation of admission policies by some schools can actually serve to discourage the enrolment of Travellers. The WSE process should continue to include enrolment policies within its remit.

7.4.3 Transfer of information
The extent to which feeder primary schools provide post-primary schools with information on the educational achievements and educational needs of their pupils as they transfer should be increased. The proposal by the NCCA that pupil report cards be introduced, for example, could be a formal vehicle for providing such information in a standardised form.

7.4.4 Retention in the post-primary system
In 2004/05 approximately 1,850 Traveller pupils were enrolled in post-primary schools. Most Traveller pupils remain in post-primary schools for one to three years, and the majority of these are participating in the junior cycle. By the age of sixteen most young Travellers have left mainstream post-primary education, with only a small minority progressing to the senior cycle.

In 2004/05 there were about 260 Traveller pupils in the senior cycle. Table 2 (chapter 3) gives the estimated numbers of Traveller pupils in post-primary schools for 2004/05, while table 3 provides data on the estimated distribution of Traveller pupils in post-primary schools in recent years. The number of Travellers in post-primary schools has been improving, with some completing the Junior Certificate and progressing to the senior cycle; but more need to be encouraged to stay to the end of the junior cycle (which equates usually with the end of compulsory education) and beyond into the senior cycle or into other education and training courses.

7.4.5 Traveller parents
The Department of Education and Science's *Survey of Traveller Education Provision* (published in May 2006) found that many Traveller parents want their children to benefit from a good education, achieve good grades in state examinations, and get meaningful and sustainable employment. However, the survey found that some parents are concerned that:

- they do not understand the complexity of the post-primary system

- their children are dropping out easily

- the system seems to be more suited to girls than boys, and they would therefore like more practical subjects

- their children are progressing poorly with literacy and numeracy, and some were not learning Irish.

The survey also found that some Traveller parents:

- do not value post-primary education very highly, as traditionally in Traveller culture boys are expected to adopt full adult male roles and responsibilities early in adolescence

- believe that barriers to their own advancement have been created because of their own limited education, problems with literacy and numeracy, and, for some, their nomadic life-style

  Such a background can affect their ability to read school brochures, notes and other communication from schools and to support their children with their homework

- find it difficult, for a variety of reasons, to approach their local post-primary school to enrol their children.

The survey is concerned:

- with the high absentee rates (often greater than 50 per cent)

- that many Traveller boys leave before completing the Junior Certificate and suggests that there is a need to consider introducing a new model, consisting of a mixture of education and training, to attract and retain male Traveller pupils

- with the low levels of competence in literacy, numeracy and general communication skills for many Traveller pupils; on the other hand, the survey found that many Traveller pupils are coping well in mainstream classes, and some are excelling

- that many Traveller pupils are attempting examination papers at foundation and ordinary levels in the Junior Certificate

- about the small number of young Travellers progressing to the senior cycle, but notes that the numbers are increasing

- that more Traveller pupils need to integrate well in primary school, as they would then be more prepared and more likely to succeed in post-primary school

- about the provision of education opportunities for young Travellers who live a nomadic life

- that more post-primary schools should welcome the enrolment of Travellers, thereby providing a wider choice of schools for young Travellers

- that school enrolment policies and practices take account of Travellers' needs and culture.

The survey recommends that Traveller parents be informed, empowered and supported in overcoming their concerns and difficulties as they seek to assist their children to achieve a high-quality, relevant post-primary education, and that schools and the system in general consider the needs of Traveller pupils.

7.5 Consultation with Traveller learners and parents, 2004

Concerns about post-primary school similar to those outlined in section 7.4 were recorded in the findings of the consultation process with Traveller learners and parents. They included:

- **Enrolment.** While many Travellers have had positive experiences in relation to the enrolment of their

children, difficulties are still being encountered by some parents in enrolling their children in certain post-primary schools, despite legislative requirements.

- **Parental concerns.** Some Traveller parents find it difficult to visit the local post-primary school and to communicate with the principal or teachers in the school. They find it daunting to visit the school to seek enrolment forms, to ask for information about the school and its curriculum, etc. Schools may not be aware of the difficulties that Traveller parents have in this regard.

- **Consideration of the Traveller viewpoint.** In some schools the curricular and administrative policies being formulated do not give due consideration to the impact they may have on Traveller parents and their children.

- **Identity.** While in school, many Traveller children experience feelings of isolation and rejection. As a result, many of them try to hide their identity so as to avoid discrimination or bullying.

7.6 Addressing the attendance, attainment and retention issues

Addressing the core issues of attendance and attainment at the primary level is essential to providing Traveller pupils entering post-primary school with a strong foundation for successful participation, attainment and retention throughout the post-primary years. A number of contributory factors affecting low levels of attendance, attainment and early school-leaving have been identified, and these include:

- negative school experiences and low expectations by some parents and pupils

- a lack of understanding of the post-primary curriculum, concerns about the content of the curriculum and the availability of different courses, the variety of post-primary personnel and the number of subjects available, different levels on offer in each subject, a lack of understanding of the role of the different types of teachers and other educational professionals (for example NEPS, NEWB), a lack of inclusion policies in schools, a lack of encouragement, a lack of positive recognition of Traveller culture and life, peer pressure, the cost of post-primary education, and difficulty with homework

- the availability of training allowances for fifteen to eighteen-year-olds in Youthreach and senior Traveller training centres and the extent to which this policy is having the unintended consequence of creating an incentive for some Traveller pupils to leave mainstream post-primary education early.

The implementation of the recommendations for addressing the core issues of attendance, attainment and early school-leaving at the post-primary level through school attendance policies and through an emphasis on improving individual levels of Traveller pupils' attainment are of critical importance to the success of Traveller education. *The Guidelines on Traveller Education in Primary Schools* (2002) and *Guidelines on Traveller Education in Second-Level Schools* (2002) provide practical advice on these issues.

Initiatives such as the VTST "Star Pupil Programme" should be expanded if Traveller pupils are to be encouraged to remain in post-primary school. (See example 10.)

Example 10: The "Star Pupil Programme"
This programme, in Tallaght, Co. Dublin, seeks to retain Traveller pupils in education up to the Leaving Certificate and to link progress in education with meaningful, paid summer work experience. On completion of their education and work experience it is expected that these pupils will be suitable for mainstream employment. Pupils are given training in the preparation of a CV and in interview skills. The programme aims to positively influence the attitude and response of employers to Travellers, to challenge the cycle of early school-leaving, and to give Traveller pupils prospects for long-term employment and to raise their expectations.

7.7 Alternatives to mainstream post-primary education

Travellers under the age of sixteen must be encouraged to stay in mainstream schools in accordance with legislative requirements. New models may be needed within the mainstream post-primary system to encourage Travellers (and other pupils) who are at present disillusioned about remaining in school. Greater flexibility may be needed, such as a greater mix of education and training options that could be run concurrently. The option of their placement in Youthreach, FÁS or other alternative integrated mainstream courses should be provided for only in exceptional circumstances and in accordance with stringently applied criteria. Such an option must be considered only following consultations with education welfare officers, representatives of the school, including the principal and guidance counsellor, the visiting teachers, the pupils, and parents. The payment of a training allowance to pupils under the age of sixteen should cease in all state-funded programmes, thereby ensuring equal treatment in all schemes.

The NCCA has prepared proposals for the reform of the senior cycle. These include offering tutorial time to all senior-cycle pupils as a support for learning, and the provision of short courses that would offer more choice and flexibility to all pupils, including Traveller pupils.

Travellers between the ages of sixteen and eighteen who may be at risk of early school-leaving should be encouraged to stay in mainstream post-primary education in the first instance. Such support might include a combination of measures, such as the Leaving Certificate - Applied, Leaving Certificate Vocational Programme, and the new integrated School Support Programme under the DEIS Action Plan. If, after due process, they are unable for some reason to stay in school, their placement in an alternative integrated course, such as Youthreach or FÁS apprenticeships, should be considered in consultation with the education welfare officers, visiting teachers, and career guidance counsellors, the pupils, and their parents.

Youthreach, in these exceptional circumstances, should be the preferred option, as it is specifically for young people, including Travellers, who have not benefited from the mainstream post-primary system.

7.8 Models of good practice

Models of good practice from education initiatives such as transfer programmes and the SCP, with its study support and holiday-time support, should be extended and made available to post-primary schools that Traveller pupils are attending. Example 11 outlines the team approach that is taken to provide Traveller pupils with an inclusive education in one post-primary school. Such an approach is to be found in many schools throughout the country.

Example 11: A team approach to inclusive Traveller education at a post-primary school
We foster a team approach to the education of all students in our community and provide a curriculum appropriate to their needs. We encourage partnership with parents and all relevant agencies in the area to ensure that our students remain in full-time education to achieve maximum academic potential, personal fulfilment, and growth.

Transfer programme
Sixth-class primary students are invited to the school induction programme following visits to the primary schools by the principal, HSCL co-ordinator, and first-year house head. Separate meetings for Traveller parents are sometimes arranged, but only at the request of the parents themselves if they want further reassurance regarding their child's welfare.

Meeting of sixth-class teachers
Principal, year head, HSCL co-ordinator, guidance counsellor, learning-support teacher and resource teacher for Travellers are all present with the primary teachers, where we share any relevant information to promote a smooth transfer for the students.

Class allocation
Students are assigned to class groups (15 max.) following short entrance assessment tests. Every effort is made to review these placements continuously, based on teacher observation and continuous testing of ability and attainment, student welfare consideration, and parental wishes.

Literacy and numeracy project
This successful approach has been developed in conjunction with the School Completion Programme (SCP) and the Junior Certificate Schools Programme (JCSP) Library Project. The library is the setting for intensive two-hour morning literacy or numeracy, with a team approach involving English and Maths teachers, learning-support teachers, resource teachers for Travellers, youth leaders from SCP, the librarian, etc.

Paired reading
One-to-one reading with the participation and encouragement of a group of parents, organised by the HSCL co-ordinator.

Laptop projects
Each student has the use of a laptop for numeracy or literacy "games", e.g. Numbershark, Wordshark (covert learning).

Visits
Authors, creative writing, animal magic - the library provides an excellent environment for visitors to engage with the students.

Awards
Students receive awards (certificates, cinema tickets, book tokens, etc.) for attendance, uniform, good work, effort, punctuality, etc.

Trips, outings, breakfast club, homework club, supervised study
Students benefit from a wide range of extracurricular activities organised in conjunction with SCP and University College, Cork, Traveller Access Programme.

JCSP
Involvement in JCSP is central to the work of the school. Students gain hugely from the very suitable class materials JCSP has developed and the various projects they have participated in, e.g. Write-a-Book, Storytelling CD.

Our visiting teacher for Travellers has always been a source of continuous support, advice and encouragement to us in our endeavours to provide an inclusive education for Travellers.

Terence MacSwiney Community College, Cork

7.9 The intercultural approach in teacher training

Schools adopting and implementing an intercultural approach in the total curriculum and in school life in general greatly benefit all their pupils, including Traveller pupils. Equality, diversity, interculturalism, anti-bias, anti-discrimination and anti-racism education and an awareness of Traveller culture and needs have not generally been dealt with in a comprehensive manner in the initial education, induction or CPD of post-primary teachers. School communities need to continue to adopt inclusive policies and to be trained in best practice to enable the inclusive school to evolve, where all its participants develop an openness to change in the inclusive school model. This will involve sustained support from the colleges of education and the departments of education in universities that train teachers, from the Department of Education and Science and in particular its Teacher Education Section, from the SDPI, from the Second-Level Support Service to ensure that subject specialist teachers adopt this approach, and from education centres and other organisations that influence teachers, including the teachers' unions, management bodies, and Traveller organisations.

School planning and the formulation of school policies in such areas as supervision, bullying, homework, outings, consultation with parents and home-school liaison should be sensitive to the particular circumstances of Traveller pupils.

7.10 Clarity of roles

A focused and co-ordinated approach will need to be adopted by the DES and its agencies, working together, to address the issues referred to above. There is a need for clarity of roles for all involved, including the support teachers (from the ex-quota allocation), for visiting teachers, for education welfare officers, for all members of the school staff, and for HSCL and SCP co-ordinators and guidance counsellors. All participants should act as a team to provide a welcoming, inclusive school that recognises Travellers' culture and needs, where Traveller pupils attend, attain and progress to completion of the senior cycle, and where Traveller parents play an active role in school activities.

7.11 Recommendations, proposed plans of action, and suggested time scale

General objective - Post-primary education

Traveller pupils should have equality of access, equality of participation and equality of outcome in a fully inclusive post-primary education system that respects Traveller identity and culture.

Post-primary education Recommendations	Proposed plans of action	Suggested time scale
Recommendation 1 **Inclusion and Enrolment:** Enrolment policies should include Travellers. Segregated education should be phased out.	1. All post-primary schools should have an enrolment policy that accords with education and equality legislation and that welcomes Travellers, celebrates cultural diversity, and promotes interculturalism. This policy should be ratified by the patrons or trustees and by the board of management.	Short term
	2. The enrolment policy should be continually evaluated to determine whether it meets the needs of all pupils, including Traveller pupils.	Short to medium term
	3. The whole-school evaluation process should continue to evaluate the inclusiveness of schools and should determine whether each school is continuing to evolve into an inclusive school.	Short to medium term
	4. Phase out the remaining three segregated educational schools for twelve to fifteen-year-old Travellers.	Medium term
Recommendation 2 **Transfer and Retention:** Support the transfer of Travellers to mainstream post-primary schools, and improve the retention of Travellers in mainstream post-primary schools.	1. The transfer of Traveller children from primary to post-primary school should increase from 85 per cent to 100 per cent within the five-year life span of the report. The NEWB, Traveller organisations, Traveller parents, VTST and local schools need to act in a co-ordinated manner to ensure that all Traveller children transfer to post-primary education.	Short to medium term
	2. Links between primary and post-primary schools need to be enhanced if Traveller pupils are to make the transfer successfully.	Short to medium term
	3. Comprehensive integrated packages to assist the successful transfer from primary to post-primary education should be available in schools (The recommendations in *Guidelines on Traveller Education in Primary Schools* (2002), *Guidelines on Traveller Education in Second-Level Schools* (2002) and the *ESRI-NCCA report* (2004) provide practical guidance.)	Short to medium term
	4. Schools should be supported in developing schemes for retaining all pupils, including Traveller pupils, for example through the availability of the SCP, JCSP, transition year, LCVP, and LCA. Consideration should be given to providing new models that include not just the academic component but also a greater emphasis on training and work experience over and above that available in transition year and LCA, for example. Such models could be more attractive to all potential early school-leavers.	Short to medium term

Post-primary education Recommendations	Proposed plans of action	Suggested time scale
	5. Sufficient guidance resources need to be provided for schools for guidance courses tailored to meet the needs of pupils, including Traveller pupils, to be developed to support active learning, provide opportunities to explore career and employment options, and facilitate transfer to further and higher education, training, and employment.	Short to medium term
	6. All pupils are required by law to stay in education until they are sixteen or to the completion of three years of the junior cycle, whichever is later. The ideal situation would be where there was 100 per cent retention to the end of the junior cycle. The present drop-out rate for Travellers is unacceptably high. For the life span of this report a targeted initiative should be taken to ensure that all pupils remain to the end of the junior cycle. Half those who complete the junior cycle should then complete the senior cycle. For this to become a reality a determined team effort by all the partners in the school - including the VTST, EWOs, HSCL, guidance counsellors, parents, and Traveller organisations - is required. In the following five years Traveller pupil retention should be on a par with that of their settled peers.	Medium to long term
	7. There should be agreement between Government agencies and other stakeholders that no allowances should be paid to young people under the age of sixteen in any schemes.	Short term
Recommendation 3 **Attendance, and linking the home and the school:** Develop the educational welfare service and other home-school supports to achieve as near full attendance as possible.	1. Effective school attendance policies will require Traveller parents (who have the primary responsibility in this regard), education welfare officers, VTST, RTTs, HSCL co-ordinators, SCP co-ordinators and Traveller organisations to work as a team to co-operate and co-ordinate in ensuring maximum attendance. The roles and responsibilities of all concerned need to be clearly set down. The educational needs of nomadic Traveller families require special attention.	Short to medium term
	2. The importance of attendance, the legislative implications and the role of the EWO should be clarified for Traveller parents and made available to them in an accessible form.	Short term
	3. By the end of the life span of this report the target for Traveller attendance should be that 100 per cent have absences of less than 20 days per year.	Medium to long term

Post-primary education Recommendations	Proposed plans of action	Suggested time scale
Recommendation 4 **Attainment:** Raise the attainment level of Traveller pupils on a par with national standards.	1. The recommendations in the STEP report should be considered to determine how attainment levels can be improved.	Short to medium term
	2. All pupils, including Traveller pupils, should have access to the full curriculum and should be encouraged to achieve to their highest capabilities.	Short to medium term
	3. Schools should continue to adopt an inclusive, whole-school approach to respond to the educational needs of all pupils, including Traveller pupils. This would involve systematic planning through the school team taking a partnership approach: principal, class teacher, learning support, pastoral care, career guidance, and counselling (starting at the junior cycle), together with VTST, HSCL, SCP, etc. Work by each member of the team should complement and reinforce that of other members. Systematic planning by the school team should take place at the level of individual pupils through establishing targets, the use of tracking systems, and regularly monitoring progress with the aim of supporting pupils in achieving their full educational potential.	Short to medium term
	4. Schools should continue to adopt an integrated learning-support system for pupils with identified educational needs. Learning support should be provided in class, where appropriate and possible, and should involve consultation between the learning-support teachers and the subject specialist teachers. Parents of pupils receiving learning support need to be regularly consulted and informed about what is involved and the benefits to be gained.	Short to medium term
	5. The NEPS should continue to develop appropriate instruments (free from cultural bias etc.) for the assessment of all pupils, including Travellers. These instruments should be made available to all schools.	Short to medium term
	6. Schools should continue to have high expectations of all their pupils, including Traveller pupils, and should encourage them to be ambitious and to achieve to the highest level possible, reflecting their capabilities. Guidance counsellors should be aware of Traveller culture and of Traveller pupils' educational needs and in first year should provide them with advice and guidance on decisions to be taken and their consequences for future options.	Short to medium term
	7. The Junior Certificate Schools Programme and Leaving Certificate - Applied should be more widely available. Other flexible models that include education, training and work experience should be considered, and criteria established.	Short to medium term

Post-primary education Recommendations	Proposed plans of action	Suggested time scale
Recommendation 5 **Training in equality and diversity:** Equality and diversity training should be a compulsory component of the pre-service, induction and CPD of teachers. It should also continue to be a component of the CPD of inspectors and the personnel of SDPI and Second-Level Support Services (SLSS).	1. Training for boards of management, trustees, patrons, teachers and principals should be provided so that they continue to have an open attitude towards Travellers, be aware of best practice, and become skilled in dealing positively with all aspects of equality and diversity, including Traveller aspects. Equality training through SDPI, SLSS and other CPD, such as training offered by education centres and by teachers' and management unions should take a whole-school, cross-curricular approach, as advocated in the NCCA's Intercultural Guidelines (2005). Equality training should emphasise not only equality and diversity but also interculturalism, anti-bias, anti-racism, and anti-discrimination. Representatives of the Traveller and other minority communities should be invited to become involved in such training. All schools should continue to evolve into inclusive schools. Other education providers, such as Youthreach and FÁS, should also receive equality training.	Short to medium term
	2. Cultural diversity should permeate the curriculum and school life, with Traveller culture and life portrayed in a positive way. Traveller culture and identity should be respected and welcomed in schools.	Short to medium term
	3. *The Guidelines on Traveller Education in Second Level Schools* (2002) and the forthcoming *Guidelines on Intercultural Education for Post-Primary Schools* (to be published by the NCCA in 2006) are and will be useful intercultural materials and resources for use in post-primary schools taking a whole-school, cross-curricular approach. Guidelines are also produced by the IVEA, LYNS and others that can also assist.	Short to medium term
	4. The Teaching Council should require that compulsory modules on equality and diversity be included in the initial training, in induction and in the CPD of all teachers.	Medium term
	5. To carry out whole-school evaluations of the inclusive school, inspectors will need continuing professional development in evaluating • equality of access, participation, and outcome • interculturalism, anti-racism, anti-bias, and anti-discrimination • inclusive practices involving Traveller pupils and procedures for monitoring attendance, attainment, and retention.	Short to medium term

Post-primary education Recommendations	Proposed plans of action	Suggested time scale
Recommendation 6 **Traveller parents:** Ensure that schools welcome, respect and support Traveller parents in becoming more involved in school life.	1. The Department of Education and Science, in consultation with the National Parents' Council, VTST, and organisations representing Traveller parents should continually encourage schools to welcome, respect and support Traveller parents. The Traveller Guidelines (2002), the NCCA's *Intercultural Guidelines* and Parent DVD and other resources should assist with this process.	Medium term
	2. Where Traveller pupils are enrolled, boards of management should continue to collaborate with visiting teachers, learning and resource teachers, HSCL and form tutors and should establish measures to facilitate Traveller parents in visiting the school and understanding its educational aims and objectives.	Short to medium term
	3. Traveller parents should be invited to become involved in a meaningful way in the post-primary school and in the education of their children, for example in consultation processes on school policy issues and on the parents' council. Traveller organisations should encourage parents to participate in this process.	Short to medium term
	4. Traveller parents and pupils should discuss available options with guidance counsellors so that they can make informed decisions and be aware of the consequences of particular decisions for the Traveller pupil later on.	Short to medium term
Recommendation 7 **School development planning:** School planning and the SDPI should have an increased emphasis on equality, on inclusion, and on the educational needs of the Travellers.	1. The school development planning team should continue to promote, through their training programme, equality, diversity and inclusion in post-primary schools.	Short to medium term
	2. School plans, where Traveller pupils are enrolled, should recognise, welcome and support all Traveller pupils and their parents and should make particular references to enrolment, successful transfer and retention of Traveller pupils in the school.	Short term
	3. School plans should reflect the educational needs of Travellers, including making provision for nomadic Travellers.	Short term
Recommendation 8 **Visiting Teacher Service for Travellers:** Review, evaluate and adapt the service, if necessary.	1. The VTST should be reviewed in the light of the introduction of new management structures in 2005, the establishment of the NEWB in 2002, the HSCL scheme, the publication of *Delivering Equality of Opportunity in Schools: An Action Plan for Educational Inclusion* (2005), and the fact that some Traveller pupils will be enrolled in post-primary schools not eligible to avail of DEIS initiatives.	Short to medium term

Post-primary education Recommendations	Proposed plans of action	Suggested time scale
Recommendation 9 **Funding:** Review the system of allocating teaching resources and capitation on the grounds of cultural identity.	1. The department should carry out an audit of the additional support, both personnel and capitation, provided to schools to cater for Travellers' educational needs. It should review the audit findings to determine the most appropriate way of allocating the funds to support Traveller pupils with identified educational needs.	Short term
	2. In principle, until the review is completed, ex-quota teachers or hours should be allocated in accordance with the identified educational needs of individual pupils and not because of their cultural identity.	Medium term
	3. Post-primary schools should be enabled to draw on funds where pupils have identified educational needs. Circular M43/99 may need to be updated if the recommendations are implemented. Special provision should be available when children, including Traveller children, with identified educational needs present themselves for enrolment in a school after 1 October each year.	Medium term
Recommendation 10 **Transport:** Provide school transport for Traveller pupils on the same conditions as for settled pupils.	1. Transport for Traveller pupils should be provided on the same conditions as for settled pupils, unless there are exceptional special circumstances, when special transport would be provided as a positive action measure.	Short to medium term
Recommendation 11 **Evaluation:** Evaluate and monitor Traveller education through the WSE process and also through subject and thematic evaluations.	1. The WSE, as part of its formal remit, should evaluate provision for Traveller pupils enrolled in a school. Subject and thematic evaluations should also consider the needs of Traveller pupils.	Short to medium term
Recommendation 12 **Special educational needs:** Provide support for Traveller pupils with identified special educational needs on the same conditions as other pupils and with sensitivity to their culture.	1. Traveller pupils should continue to be treated in the same way as all other pupils when it comes to providing support for special educational needs by SENOs and the NCSE. Traveller parents need to be made aware of this.	Short term
	2. NCSE, SENOs and NEPS officials should ensure that, in accordance with normal protocol, Traveller parents are consulted about their children's needs and that the Traveller pupils are assessed in a manner that is sensitive to their culture.	Short to medium term

Post-primary education Recommendations	Proposed plans of action	Suggested time scale
Recommendation 13 **Early school-leaving:** Support post-primary schools in meeting the needs of Traveller pupils who want to leave school early.	1. Within five years the number of Traveller pupils who complete the junior cycle should be increased to 100 per cent. In addition, there should be a target of 50 per cent for those who complete the junior cycle and go on to complete the senior cycle. To this end the new SSP should endeavour to meet the needs of pupils, including Traveller pupils, who are at risk of leaving school early. Schools not included in the new SSP should have retention schemes for all pupils, including Traveller pupils, who are at risk of early school-leaving.	Short to medium term
	2. The ultimate aim is to retain Traveller pupils in the senior cycle on a par with their settled peers.	Long term
	3. An inter-agency approach (NEWB, VTST, parents, school personnel, FÁS, Youthreach, youth workers, SSP, and career guidance officers) should be adopted to ensure that there is a managed and appropriate system for dealing with early school-leaving. This should include measures, first and foremost, to keep the pupil in school but should also cover referrals and the identification of appropriate placements for them. Stringent criteria should be developed (for example, only those with fewer than five Ds in the Junior Certificate to be accepted in Youthreach), and a tracking system should be expanded.	Short term
	4. Where a pupil under the age of eighteen wants to pursue an apprenticeship or other mainstream education or training course, this should be supported by career guidance personnel assisting the pupil to chose the most appropriate course in an integrated setting.	Short to medium term
	5. Review the allocation of allowances available in segregated courses for out-of-school Traveller pupils under the age of eighteen.	Short term
Recommendation 14 **Consultation with Traveller pupils:** A representative sample of pupils, including Traveller pupils, aged between twelve and eighteen should be consulted every two years.	1. A representative sample of pupils aged from twelve to eighteen, including Traveller pupils, should be consulted every two years to find out what they think about post-primary education, to listen to any recommendations they have, and to give them a voice as equal partners in post-primary education.	Short to medium term
	2. Traveller pupils should be encouraged to become involved in school student councils and in the local committee of the HSCL scheme.	Short to medium term
Recommendation 15 **Access to higher education:** Raise the expectations of Travellers in post-primary schools.	1. The National Office for Equity of Access to Higher Education should continue to ensure that all higher education institutions offer access programmes for schools with disadvantaged pupils, including Travellers pupils.	Short term

Post-primary education Recommendations	Proposed plans of action	Suggested time scale
	2. Traveller pupils in post-primary schools should be supported by VTST, HSCL, guidance counsellors, teachers and Traveller organisations to aspire to continue in further or higher education. Mentors, summer jobs and other initiatives, such as the Star Pupil Programme, should be used to enable these pupils to break the traditional mould and transfer to further and higher education.	Short to medium term
	3. Traveller pupils should be encouraged to pursue a career in the education system.	Short to medium term
Recommendation 16 **Data:** Data are needed to monitor transfer, attendance, attainment, and retention.	1. Transfer, attendance, attainment and retention should be monitored by parents, schools, the VTST, NEWB, DES, and others. Consideration should be given to using the post-primary pupil data-base to assist in this area. Pupils who leave the system should be identified as soon as possible.	Short to medium term
Recommendation 17 **Traveller community education workers:** Consider establishing a network of Traveller community education workers.	1. The development of community initiatives aimed at Travellers as education workers should be considered. Such workers would require appropriate training to give them the knowledge, skills and understanding required for the work. Their role vis-à-vis the VTST, HSCL and others would need to be clarified. Such initiatives should be pursued in a co-ordinated manner with other relevant agencies.	Medium term

7.12 Expected outcome

During a five-year period:

• the proportion of Traveller children transferring to post-primary education should increase from 85 to 100 per cent

• all Traveller pupils should remain in school and complete the junior cycle

• 50 per cent of those who complete the junior cycle should complete the senior cycle; full parity with the settled community should be the target of the next phase

• Traveller pupils should have equality of access, participation and outcome in an inclusive school that acknowledges and respects their Traveller identity and culture; their post-primary education should be a positive and relevant experience.

Chapter 8
Further education

8.1 Introduction

This chapter outlines the provision available for Travellers in further education and identifies concerns and challenges for the sector. It puts forward recommendations, proposed plans of action, and time scales.

8.2 Participation by Travellers in further education

The participation by Travellers in further education courses is concentrated primarily in VEC senior Traveller training centres, Youthreach programmes, and other courses and projects organised by Traveller NGOs. All adult literacy courses are open to Travellers, and of the thirty-three VECs, nineteen have specific adult literacy courses for Travellers as part of their range of literacy options. There are generally lower but growing levels of participation by adult Travellers in other adult and further education programmes, such as the Back-to-Education Initiative (BTEI).

8.2.1 Travellers and the BTEI
In the BTEI, which provides new opportunities to a wide range of adults for participating in part-time further education, 835 Travellers (or 4.5 per cent of the cohort) were involved in 2004. The BTEI emphasises learner-centredness, equality, accessibility, and inclusiveness, recognises and accommodates diversity, has quality assurance and local consultation, is innovative, and has an area-based approach.

Travellers are a particular target group of the BTEI. Outreach and pre-development work are common strategies. In a number of instances provision for Travellers is close to or on sites where they live. For example, County Dublin VEC and the City of Dublin VEC have developed specific outreach and on-site initiatives. A training allowance (including meal and travel allowances) is provided for Travellers whereby they have an entitlement to this if they are participating in full-time courses. This has proved crucial in attracting Travellers into the formal learning process. Providers engage in wide consultation with local Traveller support groups. The participation rate for Travellers is rising, and the aim would be to double the 2004 rates.

8.2.2 Senior Traveller training centres
The establishment of the present statutory model of Traveller-specific provision through senior Traveller training centres (STTCs) dates from the 1960s and 70s, a time when separate or special provision for Travellers was quite common. Many Travellers left primary school and transferred to junior and senior Traveller training

centres, if they existed in their locality. In more recent years, after a change in the rules, there is no upper age limit, and the STTCs enrol older Travellers, particularly older women.

On 31 December 2004 there were 981 trainees enrolled in STTCs throughout the country. Of this number, 81 per cent were female. However, in the under-eighteen category the proportion of males was higher; in December 2004, for example, 45 per cent of trainees under eighteen were male. A quarter of the STTC trainees in December 2004 were early school-leavers under the age of eighteen, with the remaining 75 per cent being eighteen or over. Approximately 10 per cent of trainees were not from the Traveller community.

The national network of STTCs is funded by the Department of Education and Science. The centres are managed and operated directly by the VECs. Each centre has a community-based management committee, on which the various stakeholders and support agencies are represented, that has a significant say in the running of the centre. They are mostly in disadvantaged areas, in both urban and rural communities, and in out-of-school settings. The courses are full-time and of thirty-five hours duration per week. The curriculum is broad and concentrates on integrated general education, vocational training, work experience, and personal development.

The centres offer courses that reflect the needs of the learners. Learners are provided with an opportunity to obtain FETAC certificates and to sit some subjects in the Junior Certificate and the Leaving Certificate - Applied, among others. Traveller culture is supported in the centres, and many Travellers report that they are at ease learning with their peers. Learners can follow courses in the centres for two years, but this may be extended to three years for those following an extended course, such as the Leaving Certificate - Applied. Since 2000 the STTCs have been involved in the Quality Framework Initiative developed specifically for Youthreach centres and STTCs. This initiative complements FETAC's quality assurance requirements. It involves internal centre evaluations and external validation by the Inspectorate of the Department of Education and Science.

A training allowance is paid to participants, depending on their age and attendance. Child care is also available.

The vast amount of expertise and good practice built up by staff members in the STTCs must be recognised, shared and used to ensure that a quality service is provided to adult Travellers in all courses of further education.

8.2.3 Early school-leavers

At present some Traveller early school-leavers attend STTCs, while others attend Youthreach centres. In December 2004 a census of Youthreach trainees was taken. It showed that there were 2,752 trainees, of whom 330 were Travellers. CSO figures for 2002 show that almost two-thirds of Travellers (of those who gave the age at which their full-time education ceased) left before the then statutory minimum age of fifteen, compared with 15 per cent for the population as a whole.

Lack of success at primary school is an influencing factor in early school-leaving. The focus of the NEWB at present is on the primary school, where a culture of attendance is being promoted. The solution to early school-leaving lies not solely within the primary school but also in the post-primary junior cycle. The needs of all young people, including Travellers, who are disenchanted or disengaged from primary and post-primary must be addressed, in particular by listening to them and by responding appropriately and creatively to their needs.

8.2.4 Other provision

Traveller organisations and other community development organisations have played an important role as providers of innovative learning opportunities specifically for Travellers and in outreach to the community. These initiatives have tended to emphasise community development initiatives to address issues affecting Travellers. For example, there are approximately forty primary health-care projects throughout the country, with approximately fifteen Travellers training in each project. Approximately seventy Traveller women are employed by the HSE throughout the country as community health-care workers for their community. The Primary Health Care for Travellers programme in Tullamore is an example of such a project; the services the scheme offers are outlined in example 12.

> **Example 12: Services offered by the Tullamore Primary Health Care for Travellers programme**
> Tullamore Primary Health Care for Travellers:
>
> - provides health information to the Traveller community
>
> - helps Travellers gain access to health services
>
> - networks with the Traveller community and local Health Executive
>
> - enables the Traveller community to gain access to health information

- reveals the difficulties within the Traveller community and acts as an advocate

- is involved in policy development and implementation and the monitoring of health care for Travellers

- does outreach work with Travellers about their health.

8.3 Concerns about the participation of Travellers in adult and further education

A number of concerns were expressed repeatedly in the submissions received in relation to the existing provision of services for adult Travellers. As already stated in the section on post-primary education, the availability of an alternative to school, in segregated provision - which has a number of attractions for young Travellers, such as a training allowance that supplements the family income, and the security of being with Traveller peers and friends - may have had the unintended consequence of contributing to some early school-leaving.

Concern has also been expressed that there are poor outcomes or levels of progression to employment, to further education or to training at this level. Youthreach and STTCs are monitored annually. In 2004, FETAC foundation certificates were awarded to 203 STTC trainees, 341 obtained FETAC records of achievement, 72 were awarded FETAC levels 1, 2, and 3, and 38 sat the Junior Certificate in fewer than five subjects, with 6 sitting five or more subjects. Eight sat for the Leaving Certificate - Applied. In 2004 the progression rate of trainees from Youthreach and STTCs to employment, further education or training was 75 per cent and 53 per cent, respectively.

Further concerns were raised about the impact of long-term segregated provision on relations between the Traveller and settled communities. There are also problems within the settled community when Travellers obtain employment, and with customers in retail and service outlets who do not wish to be served by a Traveller. Both these problems need to be addressed and challenged.

Other factors in early school-leaving among Travellers include a lack of provision for nomadic families, problems with accommodation, insufficient achievement at primary and post-primary levels, their distinct culture not being validated in the mainstream curriculum, and the importance of self-employment within the Traveller economy.

Other concerns expressed in the submissions received in relation to existing provision included the following:

1. There was concern that low expectations on the part of some service providers and also on the part of Traveller learners are contributing to poor outcomes.

2. There was concern that for many Travellers, being a participant on a training course or scheme becomes the only goal. Some are choosing to repeat the same course or return to centres to do other courses rather than progressing to further education or to employment.

3. There was concern that, as many adults obtaining access to second-chance education seek to achieve both educational and vocational goals, the provision of guidance services needs to be more integrated with education and training courses to provide a wide range of personally tailored supports and progression routes.

4. The scarcity of role models for Travellers progressing to further education or to mainstream employment means that expectations remain low. However, there are numerous examples of Travellers progressing to full-time employment in the community development sector, and lessons may be learnt from this.

5. While many Travellers have had positive experiences of the sector, negative attitudes can create difficulties in some learning environments. The positive experiences need to be emphasised and successful Travellers encouraged to become role models and mentors to others.

6. Approximately 10 per cent of trainees over the age of eighteen are men. A similar bias is also found for participants in adult education from the settled community. The demand for training from Traveller women is evidence of their need and desire to learn. For training schemes to be more attractive to males it may be necessary to develop new modules, such as the coppercraft course in Ennis and the landscaping training being provided by South Dublin County Council, which are more focused on employment.

The overriding concern, which was repeatedly expressed in submissions, was the need for the full inclusion of Travellers in all courses provided in institutions of further education. The opposite view has also been expressed. Many of the issues facing Travellers, such as early school-leaving and low levels of attainment, are not exclusive to Travellers. *Delivering Equality of Opportunity in Schools: An Action Plan for Educational Inclusion* (2005) aims to reduce early school-leaving and raise attainment levels. This initiative should make

significant improvements over the next five years and beyond for young people from disadvantaged communities, including Travellers, from pre-school to post-primary education (age three to eighteen) who are included in the initiative.

8.4 Literacy and numeracy

Literacy and numeracy are the foundation stones for all educational opportunities. Travellers who missed out on acquiring literacy and numeracy skills in their childhood need the opportunity to participate in an intensive education course. In particular, Traveller parents need to be encouraged and enabled to tackle their literacy needs. The VEC literacy schemes aim to address these needs. Travellers may choose mainstream literacy provision or may attend the specific courses for Travellers that nineteen VECs provide.

In the period 2004-06 the Educational Equality Initiative, phase 2, funded by the Department of Education and Science, is financing two projects, one in Co. Mayo and one in Ennis, Co. Clare, that seek to upgrade the skills of Traveller parents so that they can help their school-going children with homework and can interact effectively with their children's schools.

8.5 Challenges in further education

The heterogeneous nature of further education poses a challenge for the prospective learner wishing to avail of second-chance and adult education services. For the prospective learner there is the issue of how to obtain access to information on the range of educational courses available and to interpret how a particular course could meet individual needs. This issue applies not only to Travellers but also to learners in the wider community and particularly those from minority groups who are vulnerable to exclusion.

To assist adults in their understanding of education provision, the Adult Educational Guidance Initiative (AEGI) was established in 2001. The initiative consists of thirty-five guidance projects throughout the country and has as its aim providing a quality adult educational guidance service locally to participants in VTOS, adult literacy, BTEI and other adult and community education courses throughout the country. The AEGI projects, staffed by guidance professionals, work closely with education providers to give learning support to adults and to assist with the planning of individual career and further or higher education progression paths. This initiative, which is funded by the Department of Education and Science and managed by the National

Centre for Guidance in Education, forms part of the National Development Plan (2000-06). Locally, the AEGI projects liaise with local agencies, including FÁS. In addition, a data-base (Qualifax) giving details of all adult education courses is available and is continually being updated. It is available on the web and also in CD format.

FÁS also provides guidance services to adults through its local offices and training centres, through its National Contact Centre in Edenderry, and through the offices of its Local Employment Service. FÁS has further information about career options and employment on its web site. However, for guidance information and advice to be fully accessible for Traveller learners and other minority groups special approaches and information channels need to be developed that are respectful of particular cultural differences and can reach out to meet their educational and vocational needs.

There is a need to ensure systematic inclusion and equality for all communities, particularly those most in need and most vulnerable to direct or indirect exclusion, such as Travellers. Affirmative action may be needed to identify those most in need. The framework of the National Qualification Authority of Ireland and the standardisation of FETAC courses will ensure standards throughout the sector. The provision of equitable policies and practices for all who wish to participate in further education must continue to be promoted and monitored.

8.6 Partnership

The STTCs need to continue to look outwards and develop partnerships with the local business community, as envisaged under the revised framework for the establishment of boards of management of STTCs, which was notified to VECs in circular 48/99. Such partnerships provide work experience and may lead to permanent jobs, give a visible ladder of progression, raise expectations, and show that progressing with learning does lead to a better quality of life. An example of this is given in example 13.

Example 13: Partnership in Ennis STTC
In Ennis STTC, trainees who are preparing for the FETAC level 5 child-care certification do part of their preparation in conjunction with the County Child-Care Committee. Their placements are in mainstream child-care provision. The centre works with the Mid-Western Region Health Service Executive and has initiated a primary health-care programme for Traveller women. In the past, a number of trainees

progressed to NUIG and obtained the diploma in community development. LCA pupils do their work placement with employers in the Ennis area. The centre has received funding from the Heritage Council to assist with the development of its coppercraft programme. In addition, the centre works with a Jobs Initiative Scheme, with FÁS, Clare Youth Services, Clare Reading and Writing Scheme, Clare County Council, and the County Child-Care Committee.

Ennis STTC, unlike the national average for STTCs, had approximately 50 per cent male and 50 per cent female trainees in its 2004/05 cohort.

8.6.1 The inter-agency approach

An inter-agency approach whereby affirmative action is taken to encourage Travellers to become employed and to train using a concurrent approach is to be praised. Such an approach was taken by South Dublin County Council and is explained in example 14. This initiative was undertaken as part of a pilot initiative for the High-Level Group on Traveller Issues.

Example 14: The South Dublin County Council initiative
South Dublin County Council initiated a programme in conjunction with FÁS whereby employment was offered to twelve Traveller men in April 2005. The programme consisted of two days' work experience per week in the Parks Department and Roads Maintenance Section of the county council and three days construction skills training per week with FÁS. Of the twelve who started in April, eight completed with FETAC accreditation in September. All eight were offered full-time employment with the county council. Six Travellers have also been employed as members of the mainstream administrative staff. In addition, some Travellers are employed as temporary clerical workers, to provide them with work experience. Two of these have been offered permanent employment.

8.7 FÁS training

FÁS is committed to providing support to Travellers who are in transition from STTCs and to supporting enterprise development within the Traveller community. In 2004 slightly more than four hundred Travellers were registered with FÁS employment services. In addition, there are 300 Travellers on local training initiatives, 120 in community training centres, and 83 participating in community employment. Two social economy enterprises specifically for Travellers support ten grant-aided employees. FÁS is involved in training Traveller women to work as health-care workers in their own communities. There are now forty courses, with fifteen participants training in each course. Seventy Traveller women are employed at present by the Health Service Executive throughout the country. In addition, FÁS supports Traveller men who are engaged in work within the Traveller economy.

8.8 Community education

The *White Paper on Adult Education* (2000) acknowledges the role played by community education initiatives, particularly the role they play in relation to capacity-building and empowering marginalised communities, as it reaches large numbers of participants from disadvantaged areas, pioneers new approaches to teaching and learning in non-hierarchical, community-based settings, and takes the lived experience of the participants as a starting point.

Community education is, by its nature, open to all and is available to Travellers. For example, community education health-care and child-care courses are particularly popular with Traveller women, as are courses that deal with personal development and confidence-building. All participants, including Travellers, can participate and be accredited by FETAC when they successfully complete FETAC modules. A number of Traveller women have participated in the course leading to the Diploma in Community Development in Cork Institute of Technology. Example 15 summarises County Dublin VEC's community learning opportunities for Travellers.

Example 15: County Dublin VEC's community learning opportunities for Travellers
County Dublin VEC provides a number of community learning opportunities for Travellers. There are five Traveller support or community groups, which deal with a range of issues that affect the lives of Travellers, including communication, health care, support with education, career development, IT skill, and literacy development. While there are Traveller adults gaining access to mainstream adult education, there remains an initial preference to engage in Traveller-specific provision. County Dublin VEC works with other agencies, including FÁS, the Department of Social and Family Affairs, South Dublin County Council, Traveller support groups, the Department of Education and Science, and others. One of the main concerns is the importance of progression from one course to another at a higher level. There may be a tendency to move across rather than up, but the availability of the NQAI framework will assist in promoting progression.

8.9 Recommendations, proposed plans of action, and suggested time scale

General objective - Further education
Travellers should have equality of access, equality of participation and equality of outcome in a fully inclusive further-education system that respects Traveller identity and culture.

Further education Recommendations	Proposed plans of action	Suggested time scale
Recommendation 1 **Inclusion:** Include Travellers in all further education provision.	1. All further education services accredited by FETAC, which is under the aegis of the NQAI, are now required to have quality assurance that includes equality standards (data collection, curriculum, teacher or tutor training and attitudes, support services, etc.). STTCs should continue to quality-assure their centres.	Short to medium term
	2. Where necessary, continuing support should be given to further-education services (i.e. all those services and schemes that are aimed at the general public) to adapt their policies and practices to become accessible, relevant and welcoming of Travellers as learners and employees. Policies on equality, anti-racism, anti-bias and anti-discrimination should be available and be reflected in the provision of services. The FETAC module on interculturalism should be used as a resource.	Short to medium term
	3. More Travellers should be encouraged to become involved in the full suite of further-education courses by Traveller organisations, by further-education providers, and by community education facilitators.	Medium term
	4. All necessary steps should be taken to bring about a situation where inclusive further-education centres become not only the focal point but also the provider of further education for Travellers as part of the wider learning community in an integrated setting.	Short to medium term
	5. Evaluation tools need to be used by providers to monitor the quality of practice and to develop a system whereby incidents of discriminatory behaviour can be reported and dealt with appropriately.	Short to medium term
Recommendation 2 **Participation:** Bring Travellers into mainstream further education provision.	1. Promotional materials describing the range of provision in the further-education system should be made accessible to Travellers, and this provision should be designed in such a way as to be attractive and relevant to Travellers.	Short to medium term
	2. A joint special initiative under, for example, the National Adult Guidance Initiative and FÁS guidance and national employment services should be aimed at Travellers to assess their further-education needs and to encourage them to participate in further education.	Short to medium term

Further education Recommendations	Proposed plans of action	Suggested time scale
	3. Support should be given to Travellers to become involved in further education through, for example, mentoring and through the provision of the new FETAC level 1, 2 and 3 courses within the ten-level NQAI model. They should be supported and encouraged to remain and complete their course. During the five-year life span of the strategy, progression rates from STTCs should be improved from 53 to 75 per cent by Travellers progressing to further-education courses at a higher level, to higher education, or employment.	Short to medium term
	4. Child care is provided to participants in Youthreach, STTCs, and VTOS. It may also be available to participants in adult literacy and BTEI if the providers have creche facilities. Such child-care provision should be culturally sensitive, and training should be given to staff members in equality and diversity.	Short to medium term
Recommendation 3 **Professional development of education providers:** Upgrade the skills of providers so as to deal positively with difference.	1. Staff members in all further-education centres should continue to be trained in equality and diversity policy areas and continue to gain an understanding of and respect for Traveller culture that will be reinforced through working with members of the Traveller community. Traveller NGOs should be involved in this training.	Short to medium term
Recommendation 4 **Guidance:** Guidance professionals need training to heighten their awareness of Travellers' needs.	1. Adult guidance providers, for example the National Centre for Guidance in Education, AEGI, and others, should be aware of, understand and take account of the specific experience and needs of Travellers and other minorities that may be vulnerable to discrimination, stereotyping, and low expectations. Such support and counselling should be made accessible to Traveller learners.	Short to medium term
Recommendation 5 **STTCs:** Review the STTCs and clarify their future role.	1. An evaluation of STTCs is being undertaken by the Inspectorate of the Department of Education and Science (through collaboration between the ESRU and the Regional Offices Directorate), and an expenditure review of Youthreach and STTCs is also being undertaken. These two initiatives should, among other things, evaluate the role, function and future of STTCs, educational quality, levels of progression and ways to promote progression to mainstream provision, lower age limits, location, and the need for affirmative action. They should also take into consideration the strategic plan for developing STTCs being prepared by the Directors' Association, IVEA, NATC, CEOs' association and national co-ordinator for STTCs. The review should involve consultation with all the stakeholders.	Short term

Further education Recommendations	Proposed plans of action	Suggested time scale
	2. Most staff members in STTCs are highly qualified for their teaching role. Some may need to upgrade their skills and to obtain particular qualifications related to their employment and recent developments in the centres. Members of the staff should be encouraged and supported in this.	Medium term
	3. STTCs should not enrol young people under the age of eighteen. Mainstream provision in post-primary schools or, in exceptional circumstances, in Youthreach or FÁS should be enhanced to retain Traveller teenagers in an education and training system that is relevant to their needs.	Short to medium term
	4. No new STTCs should be opened.	Short term
Recommendation 6 **Expectations:** Increase Travellers' expectations of further education.	1. The AEGI, IVEA and AONTAS should continue to promote greater awareness among the Traveller community of existing and new opportunities in further education. Such awareness-raising should involve Traveller organisations. Traveller role models who have succeeded educationally and Traveller organisations should encourage more Travellers to become involved in further education, either directly from post-primary school or as mature students.	Short to medium term
	2. Adult Travellers should be assessed for their further education needs. In conjunction with the Department of Social and Family Affairs, FÁS, and further-education providers, an audit of their needs should be undertaken to assess their training, education and employment skills.	Medium term
Recommendation 7 **Affirmative action:** Such action, whether by community or statutory bodies, should be designed to increase the employment prospects of Travellers.	1. A collaborative effort by Traveller NGOs, IBEC, FÁS, VTST, post-primary schools, Department of Education and Science, community groups and others should ensure that pilot affirmative action programmes for placing Travellers in non-traditional employment and also in traditional employment within mainstream structures - using both an urban and a rural setting - are supported. Such affirmative action should involve an intensive tailored programme of education and training for identified Travellers, with supports, including mentoring, literacy, counselling, child care, and employment experience.	Short to medium term
Recommendation 8 **Literacy:** Deal effectively with Travellers who have a poor level of literacy.	1. NALA, AONTAS and the literacy service of the VECs should continue to encourage Travellers to train as literacy advocates and tutors in the general literacy service. This would provide positive role models, promote the value of literacy, and bring a real understanding of Traveller issues to the literacy service.	Short to medium term
	2. BTEI should be considered as a possible accelerated learning programme for literacy. Travellers should be made aware of this option.	Short to medium term

Further education Recommendations	Proposed plans of action	Suggested time scale
	3. All literacy tutors should be supported in dealing positively and effectively with all aspects of equality and diversity in the provision of their service. This should become part of the training course for all tutors.	Short term
	4. Family literacy courses should be further developed and aimed at Traveller families.	Short term
Recommendation 9 **Outreach:** Support innovative community outreach initiatives.	1. Community education should continue to provide resources to positive action initiatives at the community level. In particular, this budget should support the development of innovative responses to the emerging issues of specific minorities within the Traveller community, such as Travellers with disabilities, older Travellers, etc.	Short to medium term
Recommendation 10 **Tracking:** Collect data on Travellers' progression through the education and training spectrum.	1. Data needs to be collected so that Travellers' progression from post-primary to STTCs, to further education or elsewhere is tracked. Where necessary, if Travellers become disillusioned or drop out of an adult or further education course they should be contacted and encouraged to return and complete the course.	Short to medium term
	2. Intensive efforts are required to ensure greater progression to the broader spectrum of mainstream provision.	Short to medium term
Recommendation 11 **Partnerships:** A partnership approach is required.	1. The Department of Education and Science cannot work successfully on its own in this area. Integrated policies and practices are needed. Many other Government departments, agencies, employers, local employment services, the settled community and the Traveller community must become involved so that a holistic approach can be taken to the provision of an education service that takes account of the educational expectations of Travellers and provides for them a realistic progression into the mainstream economy - always sensitive to differences between their Traveller culture and the culture of the settled population.	Short to medium term
Recommendation 12 **Employment:** Access to employment should be a reality on the successful completion of further education.	1. During and on completion of their involvement in further education, Travellers should have access to mainstream employment appropriate to their qualifications. Employers, FÁS employment services and IBEC need to be active in this regard. Travellers should have a real expectation of a job at the end of their training and of the possibility of promotion for a job well done.	Short to medium term

8.10 Expected outcome

Within five years, the number of adult Travellers enrolled in integrated mainstream further education should significantly increase, thereby providing them with an opportunity to upgrade skills, gain accreditation, and progress to employment or to higher education. The STTCs should be reviewed and their future role clarified.

At the end of five years a review of Traveller involvement in further education should be undertaken. This review should set targets for the full integration of Travellers in mainstream further education, with the exception of targeted transitional initiatives.

Chapter 9
Higher education

9.1 Introduction

This chapter outlines the initiatives being taken to involve and increase the participation of Travellers in higher education. It puts forward recommendations, proposed plans of action, and time scales.

9.2 The higher education system

The higher education system comprises seven universities, fourteen institutes of technology, and a number of other institutions. The Universities Act (1997) requires universities to "promote access to the university and to university education by economically or socially disadvantaged people and by people from sections of society significantly under-represented". There are similar responsibilities on institutes of technology.

Higher education has a role to play in producing a more just and equal society. Until now, few Travellers have participated in higher education. Estimates suggest that fewer than 20 were at third level in 2002. In September 2004 it was estimated that 28 Travellers were enrolled in higher education. Most Travellers who participate do so under the scheme for mature disadvantaged students, while some progress directly from post-primary education. (In assessing Travellers' participation in higher education, one of the difficulties is that there is no system for collecting data on the numbers participating.)

In 1999 the Higher Education Authority invited universities and other designated institutions to develop initiatives aimed at individuals from under represented groups. The Traveller community is being addressed through the Improving Access and Progression Strand of the HEA Strategic Initiatives Scheme. In general, this initiative is co-ordinated by access officers. In 2005, €7.7 million was allocated through this scheme to eleven institutions funded by the HEA for the implementation of strategic initiatives to improve access and progression to higher education by under-represented groups of learners. This initiative was reviewed in 2004, and the report was published by the National Office for Equity of Access to Higher Education. Schemes funded by this initiative include work with primary and post-primary schools and the provision of academic courses, participation, and research. A brief summary of some of the programmes is given in the next section.

9.3 Work with the Traveller community at the primary and post-primary levels

As many Traveller children do not complete post-primary education, work with primary and post-primary schools forms an important part of access activities in the higher education institutions. A schools programme in NUIC has established links between the university and ten regional schools with significant numbers of young people from the Traveller community. Homework support groups, parenting courses, cultural awareness initiatives and an induction programme for transfer from primary to post-primary schools are offered, with all activities organised and provided by the schools. NUIC has had a number of mature Traveller students and was involved in an initiative with the Irish Traveller Movement to produce a video, *Moving On: Travellers and Third-Level Education* (2004), promoting third-level education among Travellers.

Since 2003 DCU Access Service has been working in partnership with the VTST on the development and provision of a programme aimed at pupils and parents in both primary and post-primary schools in the north Dublin area. It is aimed at improving retention and increasing awareness of educational opportunities. Several activities are concerned with broadening access for members of the Traveller community. A Traveller programme begins in fifth class and is continued throughout post-primary school. This initiative is aimed at raising awareness of educational opportunities, familiarity with the college, the creation of role models, and the involvement of parents in the pupil's educational decisions. In addition, an open day was held in the university for Traveller women, and ninety-seven attended. Traveller parent days were organised in 2004 and 2005. (See example 2.)

Trinity College, Dublin, is developing a programme promoting education opportunities and choices for fifth and sixth-class pupils and parents from the Traveller community. The initiative, in partnership with the VTST, will include a series of workshops in the college for parents.

9.4 Participation

NUIM has had a relatively high number of Travellers undertake studies in the Department of Applied Social Studies. Sixteen have completed a full undergraduate course, and of these three have gone on to full degree courses. NUIM has achieved participation through its outreach programmes and through the specific support mechanisms it has for Traveller students, including

Traveller-specific tutorials. Its emphasis up to now has been on courses that dovetail with potential involvement by Travellers in youth and community work in their own communities.

One Traveller was called to the Bar in 2005.
In NUID, eight members of a Traveller women's group completed a certificate in equality studies in 2003.

The NATC, in conjunction with NUIC, started a diploma and degree outreach course in Athlone. There are 32 participants, of whom 18 are Travellers.

The Curriculum Development Unit in Mary Immaculate College, Limerick, has developed multimedia resources to support teachers, parents, and pupils, including distance-learning materials for the Traveller community. Some members of the Traveller community have undertaken the After-School Support Educational Training (ASSET) course, which assists adults in educational work with children. Two hundred and five children from the Traveller community and the refugee community are attending after-school clubs run by ASSET-accredited facilitators. Twelve Traveller women completed the ASSET course in 2003/04 in an outreach centre in Co. Tipperary.

A women's group and a men's group participate in a Traveller access programme in the University of Limerick, assisting with completion of the Leaving Certificate for some. Some of these women students are due to progress to degree courses.

In NUIG a community outreach education initiative provides introductory development programmes, accredited courses, and advisory support services. Participation is particularly encouraged from members of the Traveller community and other marginalised groups. In 2004 thirteen Travellers participated in these courses, and a further two have progressed to full-time undergraduate studies in the university.

In 2006 the RCSI (Royal College of Surgeons in Ireland) Bursary Fund was established. Two places in medicine, two places in occupational therapy and two places in pharmacy will be set aside for Traveller students. Suitable candidates will be fully funded and supported.

9.5 Research

The *Report of the Action Group on Access to Third-Level Education* (2001) for the Department of Education and Science drew attention to the need to address educational disadvantage and the marginalised at the earliest possible level, including the pre-school level. The report also emphasised the need to build links at the local level between individual pupils, schools, and the local third-level institution. The report also proposed that a more effective range of supports be made available to students from disadvantaged and marginalised backgrounds, both before and during their participation in third-level education. It set out strategies for meeting increased participation as well as drawing attention to the issues affecting the participation of students from disadvantaged communities.

In 2002 the Higher Education Equality Unit published a report, *Creating an Inter-Cultural Campus*. This report examined a number of issues of relevance to Travellers in higher education. It suggested that there is a need to bring equality concerns to the centre of planning in order to increase the participation of minorities. Another of its recommendations is that measures be established for confronting discrimination and racism within the system. It also advocated positive actions to increase the level of participation and to support minority students while they are there.

A national forum on access for Travellers in university education was hosted by NUIM in 2003. At Mary Immaculate College, Limerick, the Learner Support Unit completed a needs analysis of Travellers and non-Irish learners in third-level education as part of its Moving On project. In conjunction with the Limerick Traveller Development Group and Mary Immaculate College, four Traveller women were trained to research Limerick Traveller children's experiences of primary school. They published a book, *Whiddin to the Gauras: Talking to Our Own,* in 2005. DCU is researching existing student participation from all minorities and aims to develop stronger links with representatives of minority groups and statutory agencies working in the area.

The National Office for Equity of Access to Higher Education was established within the Higher Education Authority in August 2003, following a decision by the Minister for Education and Science. It oversees policy and practice regarding educational access and opportunity for groups that are under-represented in higher education: those that are disadvantaged socially, economically, or culturally, those with a disability, those from the Traveller community, racial or national minorities, and mature learners. The office works with the institutes of technology, universities, and all other publicly funded institutions that offer higher education courses.

In December 2004 the National Office published *Achieving Equity of Access to Higher Education in Ireland: Action Plan, 2005-2007.* This plan identifies a number of important goals and practical actions for the next three years towards achieving greater equity of access to higher education for groups now under-represented. Travellers are a target group in this plan. The plan also illustrates how the use of quantitative and qualitative targets for achieving equity of access is essential for successful implementation and for ensuring that the necessary resources are secured and allocated effectively. The National Office will develop and agree national and institutional targets for each under-represented group, with assistance from the Central Statistics Office, the Statistics Unit of the Department of Education and Science, and the institutions. These targets will be based on improved systems of data collection. An Advisory Group has been reconvened to assist with the implementation of the action plan. A representative of Traveller organisations is a member of the Advisory Group. The National Office is evaluating existing access programmes to develop and implement a national framework of policies, initiatives and successful partnerships to widen access and to support the subsequent participation of all under-represented groups in higher education.

In April 2005 *Achieving Equity of Access to Higher Education in Ireland: The Case of Travellers* was published. The HEA provided the funds for Mary Immaculate College, Limerick, to research and publish this report. It makes a number of recommendations for achieving equity of access to higher education and for developing a best-practice model of academic support for Travellers.

While challenges remain at the primary and the post-primary level, there are also challenges for higher education that must be given priority. One of the themes that has been raised repeatedly, in both the discussions and the submissions, is the need to have Traveller role models. There is a need to transform Traveller education by breaking the mould in which Travellers see little benefit from staying in education. Having Travellers employed within the education system as teachers, as well as in other professions - as doctors, barristers, etc. - would be the best way to allay the doubts that parents and learners of all ages may have about the value of education. The positive steps being taken to increase the level of successful participation by Travellers in higher education, not solely for the benefit of those individual Travellers but also to send a clear message to the whole community that education can be of benefit, are very important.

9.6 Recommendations, proposed plans of action, and suggested time scale

General objective - Higher education
Higher education, with greater and easier access, should become a real option for Travellers.

Higher education Recommendations	Proposed plans of action	Suggested time scale
Recommendation 1 **Families:** Assist families to be more supportive and open to the idea of Traveller children going on to higher education.	1. Cultural issues often conflict with academic issues for Travellers. The Department of Education and Science, through the VTST, Career Guidance Service and HSCL, should work with families and the Traveller community in general to enable them to realise the benefits to be gained from higher education.	Short to medium term
Recommendation 2 **Access:** Obtain access to higher education through: • the conventional route • the mature route • the further education route • the positive action route	1. Provide information to Travellers about the different routes to higher education, including the conventional route, the mature route, the further education route, and positive action routes.	Short to medium term
	2. Primary and post-primary schools, through the VTST, HSCL, and post-primary guidance service, should vigorously pursue and advance the educational needs of Traveller pupils in collaboration with their parents. Access offices should provide support to schools. High expectations for the successful outcome of Traveller pupils must be created. Travellers should be advised about the consequences of subject or course choice in the junior cycle and access to higher education by guidance personnel, the VTST, or HSCL co-ordinators. Inspectors should monitor progress in this regard through the WSE.	Short to medium term
	3. Provide support to help Travellers gain access to higher education and successfully progress through higher education by one of the routes.	Short to medium term
	4. Travellers should be encouraged to choose from all the disciplines available in higher education.	Short to medium term
	5. The National Office for Equity of Access to Higher Education is developing and agreeing three-year national and institutional targets for access and for participation by under-represented groups, including members of the Traveller community. Once set, these targets should be regularly reviewed, perhaps every three years.	Medium term
	6. Access supports more finely tuned to the needs of Travellers and supported by the NEOT should be established, for example through: • area-based approaches linking Travellers with higher level institutions	Short to medium term

Higher education Recommendations	Proposed plans of action	Suggested time scale
	• the training of staff members on Traveller issues, attitudes of families to education, equality, anti-racism, anti-discrimination, and anti-bias • the provision of individual tutors or mentors • the provision of access: pre-entry courses to prepare Travellers for higher education.	
Recommendation 3 **Review:** Review all current higher-level access programmes and initiatives.	1. Review the forthcoming report of the National Office for Equity of Access to Higher Education on existing access programmes and other reports to determine where improvements can be made.	Medium term
Recommendation 4 **Ethos:** Continue to mainstream equality and diversity in higher-level institutions.	1. Equality of opportunity, as required by legislation, should continue to be mainstreamed and to include a clear emphasis on Travellers. Staff members should be provided with appropriate training, and these areas should be part of a student's higher-education experience. All should be reviewed and evaluated regularly.	Short to medium term
Recommendation 5 **Mentoring in higher education and in employment:** Provide targeted initiatives to ensure that Travellers are mentored.	1. The Department of Education and Science and the National Office for Equity of Access to Higher Education should support initiatives that support and mentor Travellers while they attend higher education. Traveller organisations should be involved in such targeted initiatives. 2. Travellers should also be mentored in mainstream employment appropriate to their qualifications. FÁS, IBEC, the ICTU, the public service etc. should be active in promoting the employment of Travellers who have successfully completed adult and further education courses. 3. Travellers should be encouraged to pursue a career in the education system.	Short to medium term Short to medium term Short to medium term
Recommendation 6 **Role models:** Traveller role models are needed.	1. Traveller graduates should be encouraged to act as role models for Traveller pupils in primary and post-primary education and to adult Travellers considering further and higher education.	Short to medium term
Recommendation 7 **Data:** Data on Travellers in higher education are required.	1. Data on Traveller students enrolled in higher-level institutions must be collected and evaluated if targets are to be realistically set and met.	Short to medium term

9.7 Expected outcome

During the five years,

- the number of Travellers gaining access to higher education directly from post-primary education or as mature students should increase

- the Traveller community should have high expectations, to break the mould and to see higher education as a real possibility.

The higher-level institutions should:

- continue to mainstream equality and diversity

- actively facilitate and encourage Travellers to enrol in higher-level institutions and in courses of their choice, to successfully engage in their courses, to graduate, and to enter the work force.

Chapter 10
Other educational issues

10.1 Introduction

This chapter briefly examines a number of areas that are relevant to Traveller education, including youth work, nomadism, disability, equality, data, detention schools, and education in prison. It also looks briefly at the role of Traveller organisations in education. It puts forward recommendations, proposed plans of action, and time scales.

10.2 Youth work

Youth work and youth services:

- are of particular importance for Travellers, given the possibilities for informal education they can offer young people who may not have an adequate formal education experience

- should not be seen as a substitute for formal education but as an important complement to it

- aim to enable young people, including Travellers, to integrate and to become active participants in their own communities and in the wider society

- help towards breaking cycles of poverty and exclusion

- provide opportunities for encouraging youth back into out-of-school informal or even formal education by providing a wide range of activities, including recreational and leisure activities, personal development, etc.

10.2.1 The Youth Work Act (2001)

The Youth Work Act (2001) provides a legal framework for the provision of youth work programmes and services by the Minister for Education and Science and the vocational education committees. Among many areas, the act provides that VECs must ensure, in co-ordination with voluntary youth organisations, that there is adequate provision of youth work programmes and services. The VECs are required to monitor and assess such programmes and services. The act also requires that particular regard be given to the youth work needs of socially or economically disadvantaged young people.

10.2.2 The National Youth Work Development Plan, 2003-2007

The National Youth Work Development Plan, 2003-2007, launched in 2003, recognises that the primary concern of youth work is with the education of young people in informal settings. This plan provides a blueprint for the development of youth work over a five-year period. Particular emphasis in the plan is placed on the provision of enhanced services for young people who are socially or economically disadvantaged, including young Travellers.

10.2.3 Grant Scheme for Special Projects for Youth

The Grant Scheme for Special Projects for Youth is a particular fund to provide out-of-school youth work programmes and services for young people in particular need, including Travellers. There are 167 projects in the scheme, of which 12 are specifically for Travellers, while other projects have Travellers enrolled in the various activities and programmes.

The Traveller-specific projects are operated by the National Association of Traveller Centres, the Traveller Youth Service, and Pavee Point. Youth work with Travellers involves consultation with local Traveller organisations and the local Traveller community, with members of that community being involved in the management of projects and in liaison with other voluntary and statutory agencies operating in the youth service sphere.

The Pavee Point youth work programme has been in existence since 1985 and is based on the critical social education model of youth work that is designed to promote the personal and social development of young Travellers. Pavee Point has identified a number of issues that affect young Travellers, including:

- lack of access to youth work services

- discrimination when trying to gain access to commercial recreational services

- an increase in drug misuse in the community

- the need to reinforce cultural identity

- poor accommodation and living conditions

- early school-leaving

- unemployment

- increased participation in decisions that influence their lives

- discrimination in the labour market.

Pavee Point's youth work programme involves national resourcing through the Traveller Youth Work Support Programme and direct work through the Rudus Project in three north Dublin sites. In addition, local Traveller organisations also provide specific projects.

10.2.4 Youth services for Travellers

The National Association of Traveller Centres develops, administers and co-ordinates the provision of youth services for Travellers nationally. The NATC works strategically with the network of STTCs at the national level. There are strong links between the provision of youth services to the Traveller community and educational and training courses. The youth work services and the educational and training courses provided within the STTC network overlap and often operate in partnership to empower Travellers.

Youth services are provided at present in twenty-four areas, and some eighteen youth workers are employed. These Traveller-specific projects have a number of common characteristics.

- They deal with young people between the ages of approximately five and twenty-five.

- They are designed to develop personal, social and educational skills.

- They provide opportunities for positive interactions within their own community and with the settled community.

- They encourage participation in mainstream education.

- They allow Travellers to develop a sense of pride in their identity and culture.

Activities include summer projects, educational and developmental initiatives, recreational activities, young men's and young women's groups, a drop-in service, a homework educational support service, and others.

10.3 Nomadism

10.3.1 Background

Nomadism is an important part of Traveller culture and identity. Travellers retain a specific attitude towards travel that continues to distinguish them from settled people. Some Travellers live a nomadic life for part of the year, for social and family reasons, to attend festivals and other events. Nomadism is a vibrant, dynamic process and remains an important part of cultural identity for Irish Travellers, whether they themselves are nomadic or not. Many Travellers retain an aspiration to travel; but the provisions of section 24 of the Housing (Miscellaneous Provisions) Act (2002) makes travel difficult. The loss of traditional halting sites and a lack of transient halting sites militates against a nomadic life-style.

10.3.2 Provision in other countries

Provision is made for nomadic children through a number of models, including distance learning, whereby education is provided by correspondence. Children have a base school. When they travel, schemes of work are designed for each individual child, and this keeps them in touch with the base school. It thus enables the children to retain their life-style, remain with their family, and have a relatively uninterrupted education.

10.3.3 ICT and distance learning: video-conferencing, internet, e-mail

The European Federation for the Education of Children of Occupational Travellers has developed three distance-learning pilot schemes. If successful, these schemes could lead to a more flexible pedagogy and could support the education and life-style of nomadic Traveller families. These schemes all are dependent on training and on the support of parents, who often themselves have poor literacy skills. The model could lead to education not only for the children but also for the parents.

This model requires a base school. The Trapeze project, for example, uses an audio-conferencing session once a week to provide an opportunity for collaborative work and to allow children to interact with each other, to work together, and hopefully to form friendships.

The Scottish paper *Inclusive Educational Approaches for Gypsies and Travellers within the Context of Interrupted Learning: Guidance for Local Authorities and Schools* (2003) sets out the background to interrupted learning. It observes that:

- difficulties are encountered by many learners who experience interruptions to their school education

- there is a mismatch between their particular requirements and what is generally made available within statutory provision

- there is a need to review existing practices in order to ensure that equality of opportunity is given emphasis

- there is a need to adopt more flexible approaches in the provision of services and to work in partnership with families, wherever they stay or however transitory within an area.

10.3.4 Issues for nomadic Traveller families

In accordance with the Education Act (1998) and the Education (Welfare) Act (2000), every child, regardless of their family background, should have the best possible educational start in life. Nomadic families have all the same barriers as non-nomadic Travellers, including discrimination, but they have the added disadvantage of frequently changing schools. A nomadic life makes access to the existing education system very difficult, because it reflects the structure and needs of the majority non-nomadic population.

Mobility in life-style leads to interrupted learning. Levels and patterns of mobility differ, both between and within the different groups of Travellers. Some may attend a school only once, others may enrol for a period each year or even make several visits to the same school within the one year.

For the families there is constant tension between maintaining their life-style and culture and participating fully in education. Nomadic families value financial independence, self-employment, and the ability to operate successfully as a family unit. The issues for nomadic Traveller families and the education of their children include enrolment, address, contact point, NEWB attendance requirements, uniforms, textbooks, school year versus travelling year, continuous assessment, schools valuing and understanding nomadism, and the need for teachers from the supply panel to deal with nomadic pupils, as necessary.

The existing education system does not easily respond to or facilitate the nomadic life that a small group of Travellers live. However, consideration should be given to determining how the system could facilitate nomadic pupils. Perhaps nomadic movement planned by the family, when discussed with service providers in education, could be accommodated successfully if nomadic children had a designated base school. As they travel, distance learning could provide possible options for a child's uninterrupted education. Such an approach needs to be considered.

10.4 Disability

10.4.1 The Education for Persons with Special Educational Needs Act (2004)

Since the Education for Persons with Special Educational Needs Act (2004) has been enacted the Department of Education and Science has been implementing measures to ensure that services are developed and provided for all pupils with special needs arising from a disability. The act also allows for the provision of such services in accordance with assessed need and, insofar as it is appropriate in an inclusive setting, the involvement of parents or guardians, the availability of an appeals process, and co-ordination between the health executive, education services, and other bodies.

10.4.2 The National Council for Special Education

The National Council for Special Education was established in 2003 as an independent statutory body with responsibilities as set out in the National Council for Special Education (Establishment) Order. The establishment of the NCSE is a further step towards ensuring that the requirements of children with special educational needs are identified and the necessary resources made available in a timely and effective manner.

Since September 2004 the NCSE has appointed seventy-five special education needs organisers, who are based throughout the country, with at least one organiser in each county. Each SENO is responsible for the primary and post-primary schools in their area. Placing organisers in the locality enables them to work with the parents and the schools and to co-ordinate services at the local level. Therefore, when a child has been identified as having special needs, the services can be made available as soon as possible. The advent of the NCSE is ensuring that all children with special educational needs receive the support they require, when and where they require it.

10.4.3 Allocations from September 2005

A new system for the allocation of resource teachers, begun in September 2005, involves a general allocation for all primary schools to cater for pupils with higher-incidence special educational needs, as the pupils are distributed throughout the country. This system also applies to those with learning-support needs (i.e. functioning at or below the 10th percentile on a standardised test of reading or mathematics, or both). The model was constructed so that allocations are based on pupil numbers, taking into account the differing needs of the most disadvantaged schools and the evidence that boys have greater difficulties than girls. The advantages of this general allocation are that:

- it facilitates early intervention, as the resource exists in the school when the child enrols

- it reduces the need for individual application and supporting psychological assessments

- it provides resources more systematically, thereby giving schools more certainty about their resource levels

- it gives more security to special-education teaching posts and makes special-education teaching a more attractive option

- it allows flexibility to the school management in the employment of resources, leading to a more effective and efficient provision of services

- it will adjust a school's general allocation on the grounds of a substantive changing enrolment

• it gives resources based on pupil numbers in a school and is not based on identity or other criteria.

For pupils with lower-incidence disability, resources will continue to be allocated as a result of individual applications. These pupils are not evenly distributed among schools, and so it will be the responsibility of the NCSE and the SENOs to evaluate and respond to individual applications and inform the school of the outcome.

Traveller children with identified educational needs are entitled to the services of the NCSE in the same way as all other children.

10.5 Equality

The equality legislation prohibits discrimination on nine grounds: gender, marital status, family status, sexual orientation, religion, age, disability, race, and membership of the Traveller community.

Travellers, as noted in section 1.2, are not a homogeneous group. As with the settled community, they may experience multiple forms of discrimination and so have a number of different special needs. For example, Traveller women experience discrimination both as women and as Travellers. This report has looked at membership of the Traveller community and at disability. Other areas where it is evident that difference exists are those of age and sex. For example, the census in 2002 found that two-thirds of the Travellers who gave the age at which their full-time education ceased left before the then statutory minimum age of fifteen. Many adult Travellers, therefore, have had little formal education.

Where adult Travellers have returned to education it is mostly Traveller women who have done so. In general, women constitute more than 80 per cent of trainees at the STTCs; very few adult men are returning to education. Some STTCs have a better balance, for example in Ennis.

10.6 Positive affirmative action

The Equal Status Act (2000) and the Equality Act (2004) both allow for "positive action" to be taken to ensure full equality in practice. Therefore, in the implementation of this report's recommendations it may be necessary to provide positive-action initiatives to allow specific groups of Travellers gain the knowledge, understanding, skills and attitudes necessary to enhance their opportunities within the mainstream

spectrum of lifelong learning. These affirmative-action measures should not be long-term or institutional in nature but instead should be seen as interim, transitional steps to the achievement of full participation in mainstream education.

While many positive-action measures should be provided through community organisations, statutory bodies must also recognise their obligation to take appropriate action where necessary. Positive action should concentrate on building the capacity of Travellers to become involved in other mainstream education initiatives.

10.7 Data

In the education system, as in many other areas, data specific to Travellers are not collected at present for publication. The 2002 census is leading in this area. Pavee Point is working with two hospitals to determine how best to obtain data on Travellers and on other minority groups. In addition, the Department of Education and Science is funding Pavee Point to research appropriate mechanisms for monitoring education access, participation and outcome for Traveller boys and girls in two primary and two post-primary schools. This research will make recommendations on data collection and will inform policy in this area. The inclusion of a Traveller identifier in the post-primary and primary data-bases of the Department of Education and Science is now under consideration. Other education sectors need to determine the best way of collecting data to determine how Travellers are gaining access to, participating in and progressing through education and training. In all instances, Travellers should have the option of self-identification where such data are being sought within an equality framework.

10.8 Detention schools and education in prison

There are five detention schools that provide residential care, education and rehabilitation for young people up to the age of sixteen. These young people are either remanded or committed to these schools by the courts. The Department of Education and Science does not compile statistics on the number of young Travellers who are referred. Department statistics are based on the source of referral, either remand or committal by the courts or placed by virtue of the Health Acts.

The Prison Service does not collect data specific to Travellers. A comprehensive education service is provided to all prisoners, as education has a crucial role to play in the management and rehabilitation of prisoners. Education units in prisons devise student-centred individualised courses for learners based on a broad adult education orientation. A serious literacy problem has been identified within the prison system by Morgan and Kett (2003).

10.9 The role of Traveller organisations in education

There are four national Traveller organisations. (See section 3.16 for a brief summary of each organisation.) Their involvement in Traveller education is referred to throughout this report. Their future involvement in putting forward the Traveller viewpoint is vital and is formally acknowledged through their membership of the ACTE. Among many roles, they inform the Traveller community at the basic level, are involved in training initiatives for Travellers and for the settled community, develop resources, and are partners with the department and its agencies in a number of education initiatives.

As members of the ACTE, the Traveller organisations will play an important role in advising on and evaluating the progress of Traveller education as the recommendations, having been considered and approved by the Minister, are implemented.

10.10 Recommendations, proposed plans of action, and suggested time scales

General Objective - Other educational issues

Recommendations	Proposed plans of action	Suggested time scale
Recommendation 1 **Youth work:** Continue to encourage young Travellers to become involved in youth work.	1. Continue to develop local inter-agency links between youth work projects and the formal education system, so that Travellers who are early school-leavers are encouraged back into mainstream education or training.	Medium term
	2. If a Traveller leaves school early, a formal referral system should be activated that involves consultations with the early school-leaver, their parents, guidance counsellors, VTST, HSCL, SCP, principal, EWO, and others. Progression routes back into education or training should be developed through Youthreach, FÁS, youth work providers, and mainstream education providers.	Short to medium term
	3. A review of youth work provision to which young Travellers have access should be made. The review should determine whether it is enabling young Travellers to develop their confidence and self-esteem, be challenged, and become active participants in their own communities and in the wider society.	Short to medium term
	4. Travellers should be involved in youth projects that are inclusive and not segregated, unless a specific affirmative initiative is considered necessary.	Short to medium term
	5. Youth work organisers should continually evaluate their Traveller members to determine how best to address an individual's needs.	Continuously
	6. All youth work centres should have policies on equality and diversity, and all youth workers should be trained in the implementation of these policies. Mechanisms should be established for reviewing and evaluating the implementation of these policies.	Short term
Recommendation 2 **Nomadism:** Nomadic Travellers require specific education provision.	1. The Department of Education and Science, VTST, HSCL, and NEWB, with the Department of the Environment, Heritage and Local Government, should share data on the number of nomadic Traveller families and children, to ensure that quality education services can be provided.	Short term
	2. Examine projects in other countries that use ICT as a tool for educating nomadic Traveller children.	Short to medium term

Recommendations	Proposed plans of action	Suggested time scale
	3. Examine how the VTST and the whole school team can provide an uninterrupted education for all nomadic children. This could include the establishment of a tracking system.	Short to medium term
	4. In consultation with the parents, establish a base school for each nomadic child, examine the best way to provide capitation, and determine how the educational needs of nomadic Traveller children can best be provided for and how educational data on pupils can be transferred from school to school.	Short to medium term
	5. Formal links with Northern Ireland and Britain need to be developed to cater for the educational needs of some nomadic Travellers who travel between countries.	Short to medium term
	6. Nomadic parents need to be provided with support to enable them to be responsible and to become involved in their children's education.	Short to medium term
	7. The department needs to have a response mechanism for assisting schools where nomadic children enrol during the academic year.	Short to medium term
Recommendation 3 **Disability:** Providers of education to Travellers with disabilities should be sensitive to their particular needs.	1. Traveller parents need to be provided with the information to enable them to obtain access to the NCSE and its SENOs, if necessary.	Short term
	2. Train special-education specialists who provide Traveller children with services to be sensitive to Traveller culture.	Short to medium term
	3. Traveller parents - as do all parents - need to be kept informed of their child's progress if they have special educational needs.	Short to medium term
	4. Provision should be based on need and not identity.	Short to medium term
Recommendation 4 **Equality:** Positive action initiatives may be needed for specific groups of Travellers.	1. There may be a need for some positive-action initiatives to select specific groups within the Traveller community so as to enable them to obtain the knowledge and skills needed to gain access to mainstream education and training.	As needs are identified
Recommendation 5 **Data:** Data are needed to determine whether the implementation of the recommendations is succeeding.	1. Review the collection of data from Traveller initiatives.	Short to medium term
	2. Data are needed, and the Department of Education and Science and education providers should collect data, within an equality framework.	Short to medium term

Recommendations	Proposed plans of action	Suggested time scale
Recommendation 6 **Detention schools and education centres in prisons:** Service providers need to be aware of the specific educational needs of Travellers.	1. Detention schools and prisons with Travellers need to be aware of their specific needs.	Short to medium term
	2. Policies on diversity and equality need to be adopted, implemented, and evaluated. Staff members should be provided with training to ensure that they understand and can respond to the specific needs of Travellers.	Short to medium term
Recommendation 7 **Traveller organisations:** Traveller organisations, as education partners, have an important role to play in helping to provide an improved educational outcome for Travellers.	1. National Traveller organisations should continue to be represented on the ACTE to advise and evaluate the implementation of the recommendations.	Short to medium term
	2. Traveller organisations need to be given the appropriate resources to enable them to support the implementation of specific aspects of the strategy.	Short to medium term
	3. Traveller organisations should continue to be involved in the development and provision of innovative community education initiatives.	Short to medium term
	4. Resources should be identified for specific positive-action initiatives as such initiatives are being developed.	Short to medium term

10.11 Expected outcome

All the themes described above should be evaluated and plans implemented to ensure that Travellers receive a quality, inclusive education that is mindful of their particular needs.

Chapter 11
Conclusions and recommendations

11.1 Introduction

This chapter provides a summary of the objectives, recommendations and outcomes in the report. It also sets out how it sees the future for Travellers in education and in general.

11.2 Traveller education

The Department of Education and Science is fully committed to ensuring that Travellers receive a high-quality, integrated education from early childhood to adult education that, as described in the department's mission statement, will enable individuals to achieve their full potential and to participate fully as members of society, and contribute to Ireland's social, cultural and economic development.

In the last ten years the department has provided significant additional funding for Traveller education. This additional provision is described in this report, and recommendations for future provision are made.

This report should be seen as one that provides an impetus for moving from what was historically a negative experience for Travellers to what is now provided and towards what is most desired. It should be seen as a catalyst for change. The time span envisaged in this report is five years.

11.3 The inclusive approach

For the purpose of clarity of presentation, the report is presented in discrete chapters, each dealing with one aspect, for example parents, or particular sectors of education. This structure might give the impression that Traveller education itself can be divided into discrete sectors. Such an impression would be misleading. The opposite viewpoint - of an inclusive, holistic approach to dealing with all aspects of Traveller education concurrently, in an intercultural manner - is what is proposed and is required. Success for Travellers' education requires their education, whether at pre-school or at higher education, to be a quality education that is available throughout the lifelong learning spectrum.

This report, although dealing with Travellers, is mindful of the need for a holistic approach to education in general and realises that recommendations made here are also relevant to other minority groups. For example, the need for an awareness of Traveller culture should be included in a broader intercultural framework, which acknowledges and respects in a complementary way all cultures.

The report provides:

- general objectives

- recommendations

- proposed plans of action for each recommendation

- a time scale

- expected outcomes.

It also suggests some targets; and a number of generic themes run throughout the report. These are discussed below with regard to the framework of the National Action Plan Against Racism.

The future for Traveller education requires not only the inclusive approach but also a recognition of the importance of leadership, of appropriate structures, and of the need for resources. Subject to the approval of the Minister for Education and Science, it is recommended that an implementation plan be prepared.

11.4 General objectives of the report

The general objectives for Traveller education are specified throughout the report and are summarised below.

- **Traveller parents:** Traveller parents should benefit from a comprehensive and inclusive programme of community-based education initiatives that will enable them to understand the education system, to participate in it, and to further support their children in education.

- **Early-childhood education:** Traveller children should have access to an inclusive, well-resourced, well-managed, high-quality early-childhood education, with an appropriately trained staff operating in good-quality premises.

- **Primary, post-primary, adult and further education:** Travellers should have equality of access, equality of participation and equality of outcome in a fully inclusive education system that respects Traveller identity and culture while they are participating in the primary education system, the post-primary system, and the adult and further education system, where Traveller learners will have the same chances as their settled peers and have real-life options for progression and employment on completion of their studies.

- **Higher education:** Higher education, with greater and easier access, should become a real option for Travellers.

11.5 Recommendations

The recommendations in this report are restated below. (The proposed plans of action and the suggested time scales for each recommendation are given in the relevant chapters.)

11.5.1 Recommendations for parents (from chapter 4)

Traveller parents' education: Meet the educational needs of Traveller parents.

Community development: Build Traveller parents' understanding and value of education and their direct engagement with the system.

Traveller representation: Get Traveller parents involved in the representative structures.

Parent-teacher communication: Build effective communication between Traveller parents and teachers.

School-parent relationship: Traveller parents should be included in all aspects of school life.

An inter-agency approach: This approach is required to respond effectively to Traveller parents' educational and other needs.

11.5.2 Recommendations for early-childhood education (from chapter 5)

Structures: Create a mechanism in the Department of Education and Science for administering the provision of pre-school and early-childhood education.

Inclusion: Change the grounds on which pre-school education to Travellers is provided to an inclusive, integrated service.

Availability and take-up: Increase the availability and take-up by Traveller children of pre-school education.

Quality education: Improve the quality of education available in pre-schools.

Equality: Increase the emphasis on equality in the planning and provision of early-childhood education services, and eliminate the potential for discrimination and racism.

Recruitment of Travellers: Increase the number of Travellers who are employed in the provision of early-childhood education services in a sustained and active manner.

Location and future development: No new segregated Traveller pre-schools should be established.

11.5.3 Recommendations for primary education (from chapter 6)

Inclusion: End all segregated provision at the primary level.

Enrolment: Make the inclusion of Travellers an explicit part of the school plan and also of enrolment and other policies.

Attendance: Develop the education welfare service and other home-school support to achieve as near full attendance as possible.

Attainment: Raise the attainment level of Traveller children to be on a par with national standards.

Training: Equality and diversity training should be a compulsory component of the pre-service, induction and Continuing Professional Development (CPD) of teachers. It should continue to be a component of the CPD of inspectors and of the personnel of the School Development Planning Initiative (SDPI) and Primary Curriculum Support Programme (PCSP).

Resource teachers for Travellers: Short-term and medium-term recommendations are made on the grounds that educational needs, rather than Traveller identity, should be a trigger for additional resources.

Visiting Teacher Service for Travellers: Review, evaluate and adapt the service, if necessary.

Traveller parents: Parents should be encouraged and supported to take an active part in all aspects of school life.

School development planning: School planning and the School Development Planning Initiative (SDPI) should have an increased emphasis on equality, on inclusion, and on the educational needs of Travellers.

Funding: The provision of additional funding specifically for Travellers should be reviewed.

Transport: School transport should be provided on the same conditions as for settled pupils.

Evaluation: Evaluate and monitor provision for Travellers in the primary system through the whole-school evaluation process.

Traveller community education workers: Consider establishing a network of Traveller community education workers.

Other issues: Nomadism, culture, data collection, access to homework clubs, consultation with pupils and access to higher education all need to be addressed.

11.5.4 Recommendations for post-primary education (from chapter 7)

Inclusion and enrolment: Enrolment policies should include Travellers. Segregated education should be phased out.

Transfer and retention: Support the transfer of Travellers to mainstream post-primary schools, and improve the retention of Travellers in mainstream post-primary schools.

Attendance, and linking the home and the school: Develop the educational welfare service and other home-school supports to achieve as near full attendance as possible.

Attainment: Raise the attainment level of Traveller pupils to be on a par with national standards.

Training in equality and diversity: Equality and diversity training should be a compulsory component of the pre-service, induction and CPD of teachers. It should also continue to be a component of the CPD of inspectors and the personnel of SDPI and Second Level Support Services (SLSS).

Traveller parents: Ensure that schools welcome, respect and support Traveller parents in becoming more involved in school life.

School development planning: School planning and the SDPI should have an increased emphasis on equality, on inclusion, and on the educational needs of the Travellers.

Visiting Teacher Service for Travellers: Review, evaluate and adapt the service, if necessary.

Funding: Review the system of allocating teaching resources and capitation on the grounds of cultural identity.

Transport: Provide school transport for Traveller pupils on the same conditions as for settled pupils.

Evaluation: Evaluate and monitor Traveller education through the WSE process and also through subject and thematic evaluations.

Special educational needs: Provide support for Traveller pupils with identified special educational needs on the same conditions as other pupils and with sensitivity to their culture.

Early school-leaving: Support post-primary schools in meeting the needs of Traveller pupils who want to leave school early.

Consultation with Traveller pupils: A representative sample of pupils, including Traveller pupils, aged between twelve and eighteen should be consulted every two years.

Access to higher education: Raise the expectations of Travellers in post-primary schools.

Data: Data are needed to monitor transfer, attendance, attainment, and retention.

Traveller community education workers: Consider establishing a network of Traveller community education workers.

11.5.5 Recommendations for further education (from chapter 8)

Inclusion: Include Travellers in all further education provision.

Participation: Bring Travellers into mainstream further education provision.

Professional development of education providers: Upgrade the skills of providers so as to deal positively with difference.

Guidance: Guidance professionals need training to heighten their awareness of Travellers' needs.

STTCs: Review the STTCs, and clarify their future role.

Expectations: Increase Travellers' expectations of further education.

Affirmative action: Such action, whether by community or statutory bodies, should be designed to increase the employment prospects of Travellers.

Literacy: Deal effectively with Travellers who have a poor level of literacy.

Outreach: Support innovative community outreach initiatives.

Tracking: Collect data on Travellers' progression through the education and training spectrum.

Partnerships: A partnership approach is required.

Employment: Access to employment should be a reality on the successful completion of further education.

11.5.6 Recommendations for higher education (from chapter 9)

Families: Assist families to be more supportive and open to the idea of Traveller children going on to higher education.

Access: Obtain access to higher education through

- the conventional route

- the mature route

- the further education route

- the positive-action route.

Review: Review all current higher-level access programmes and initiatives.

Ethos: Continue to mainstream equality and diversity in higher-level institutions.

Mentoring in higher education and in employment: Provide targeted initiatives to ensure that Travellers are mentored.

Role models: Traveller role models are needed.

Data: Data on Travellers in higher education are required.

11.5.7 Recommendations for other educational issues (from chapter 10)

Youth work: Continue to encourage young Travellers to become involved in youth work.

Nomadism: Nomadic Travellers require specific education provision.

Disability: Providers of education to Travellers with disabilities should be sensitive to their particular needs.

Equality: Positive action initiatives may be needed for specific groups of Travellers.

Data: Data are needed to determine whether the implementation of the recommendations is succeeding.

Detention schools and education centres in prisons: Service providers need to be aware of the specific educational needs of Travellers.

Traveller organisations: Traveller organisations, as education partners, have an important role to play in helping to provide an improved educational outcome for Travellers.

11.6 Specific target-setting

Specific targets are suggested throughout this report. These should be achieved within the suggested five-year life span. A number of these targets are listed below.

1. Increase grants to Traveller pre-schools from 98 to 100 per cent, and bring equipment grants into line with those allocated to Early Start centres.

2. 50 per cent of Traveller pre-schools should be amalgamated with mainstream early-childhood care and education provision.

3. The recommendations in the ESRU report on pre-schools for Travellers should be implemented.

4. No new segregated Traveller pre-schools should be established.

5. All pupils in primary and post-primary schools, including Traveller pupils, should have an absence of less than twenty days per year.

6. Additional resources should not be provided on the grounds of Traveller identity but in accordance with identified educational need.

7. The enhanced capitation funding provided for Traveller children over the age of twelve attending primary schools should cease.

8. The one remaining special primary school for Travellers should be closed over an appropriate period, as should the three centres that cater for Travellers aged between twelve and fifteen.

9. Training in equality and diversity for educators and others involved in the provision of education, from pre-school to higher education, should be an urgent priority.

10. Transfer from primary to post-primary education should increase from 85 to 100 per cent.

11. 100 per cent of Traveller pupils should complete the junior cycle, and 50 per cent of these pupils should remain at school and complete the senior cycle.

12. A representative sample of young people in primary and post-primary schools, including Travellers, should be consulted every second year.

13. The payment of allowances to under-sixteens should cease.

14. No Travellers under the age of eighteen should be enrolled in STTCs.

15. Progression to further education and training should increase for Travellers in STTCs from 53 to 75 per cent.

11.7 Expected outcome

For most of the chapters an expected outcome is given. These are restated below.

11.7.1 Principle of inclusion (from chapter 2)

The principle of inclusion has consequences for everyone involved in education, including the Department of Education and Science, policy-makers, teacher educators, school management authorities, teachers' unions, professional organisations, parents' representative bodies, Traveller organisations, parents (both Traveller and settled), school principals, teachers, and pupils. In the implementation of the recommendations the principle of inclusion should continue to become a reality within the full spectrum of the education system, from pre-school to adult education.

11.7.2 Traveller parents (from chapter 4)

The education system has to continue to evolve into an inclusive one that welcomes diversity in all its forms, including the Traveller community. In this regard, Traveller parents should:

- have a greater understanding of the value of education and of the education system

- participate in education, if they wish

- have high educational expectations for themselves

- continue to have high educational expectations for their children and encourage them to continue beyond compulsory education

- participate more fully in the education of their children.

Education providers should:

- engage actively with Traveller parents by including them as active partners in the education system.

11.7.3 Pre-school provision (from chapter 5)

Within the five-year span,

- half the segregated pre-schools for Travellers should be integrated, and all should be integrated within ten years, where possible

- Traveller children should have access to an inclusive, well-resourced, well-managed, high-quality, publicly funded early-childhood education, with an appropriately trained staff (including representatives of the Traveller community), operating in quality premises

- the CECDE quality framework and the NCCA's Framework for Early Learning should have been approved and implemented and should be the quality standard or mark in all pre-schools and other early-learning settings.

11.7.4 Primary schools (from chapter 6)

All Traveller children attending primary school should have equality of access, participation and outcome in a school that is fully inclusive. Schools should:

- have high expectations for the educational outcome for Traveller children

- provide information to Traveller parents on life in their school, using media that are accessible; Traveller parents should be encouraged to take an active part in all aspects of school life

- continue to provide all children, including Traveller children, who have identified educational needs with additional learning support in an integrated setting

- adopt a team approach to improving attendance by setting targets and monitoring progress.

11.7.5 Post-primary schools (from chapter 7)

During a five-year period:

- the proportion of Traveller children transferring to post-primary education should increase from 85 to 100 per cent

- all Traveller pupils should remain in school and complete the junior cycle

- 50 per cent of those who complete the junior cycle should complete the senior cycle; full parity with the settled community should be the target for the next phase

- Traveller pupils should have equality of access, participation and outcome in an inclusive school that acknowledges and respects their Traveller identity and culture; their post-primary education should be a positive and relevant experience.

11.7.6 Further education (from chapter 8)

Within five years, the number of adult Travellers enrolled in integrated mainstream further education should significantly increase, thereby providing them with an opportunity to upgrade skills, gain accreditation, and progress to employment or to higher education. The STTCs should be reviewed and their future role clarified.

At the end of five years a review of Traveller involvement in further education should be undertaken. This review should set targets for the full integration of Travellers in mainstream further education, with the exception of targeted transitional initiatives.

11.7.7 Higher education (from chapter 9)

During the five years,

- the number of Travellers gaining access to higher education directly from post-primary education or as mature students should increase

- the Traveller community should have high expectations, to break the mould and to see higher education as a real possibility

The higher-level institutions should:

- continue to mainstream equality and diversity

- actively facilitate and encourage Travellers to enrol in higher-level institutions and in courses of their choice, to successfully engage in their courses, to graduate, and to enter the work force.

11.7.8 Other educational issues (from chapter 10)
All the themes described above should be evaluated and plans implemented to ensure that Travellers receive a quality, inclusive education that is mindful of their particular needs.

11.8 Integration of services

The recommendations of the High-Level Group on Traveller Issues will be important in influencing how the proposed strategy succeeds. This group, established under the aegis of the Cabinet Committee on Social Inclusion, seeks to ensure that the relevant statutory agencies involved in providing the full range of services to Travellers would concentrate on improving the integrated provision of such services. The work of the High-Level Group supports the greater integration, cohesion and co-ordination of services and policy within the education system and between Government departments and other agencies, thereby enhancing the services provided to Travellers.

11.9 Generic themes

A number of generic themes cut across the recommendations and plans of action throughout this report, one example being training. *The National Action Plan against Racism* (2005) has a framework with five main objectives:

- protection

- inclusion

- provision

- recognition

- participation.

This framework provides a tool for considering the generic themes within the totality of the education system. The use of such an inclusive framework should help with the successful implementation of the recommendations. The involvement of all the partners in a situation where the providers and recipients, operating in an inclusive educational environment, understand each other's needs and gain positively from mutual experiences is also vital to success.

1. **Protection - An inter-agency approach**
   The Department of Education and Science, its regional offices, other agencies and education providers alone cannot successfully create, implement and review a Traveller education strategy unless all the other partners play their part in providing services to Travellers that make it conducive for them to become active participants in education. The importance of links between education and other aspects of Travellers' lives, such as health, accommodation, employment, social welfare benefits, medical cards, and social status, would be difficult to overstate. Representation from the Traveller community, through the Traveller organisations, is vital to the success of this approach. Traveller organisations have an important role to play in facilitating progress if the needs, aspirations and experiences of Travellers are to be understood. Such an inter-agency approach will benefit Travellers in gaining access to, participating in, progressing through and benefiting from the education system at all levels.

   Legislation
   Travellers are protected in equality legislation and are entitled in education legislation, as is the whole population, to a quality lifelong education service.

2. **Inclusion - Equality and diversity**
   In the medium to longer term all mainstream education will strive to be inclusive and available to all pupils, including Travellers, in a way that welcomes diversity and respects both Traveller and settled cultural identities. For this to become a reality all providers of education services and all trainers of education providers:

   - must have policies on equality and diversity in accordance with legislation

   - must build capacity by providing equality and diversity training for all their management and staff members, boards of management, trustees, patrons, and other partners.

     This training would deal with such issues as anti-racism, interculturalism, anti-bias, and anti-discrimination. It would provide the participants with the skills with which to deal positively not only with Travellers but with all aspects of equality and diversity in the provision of their particular educational service.

- must include equality and diversity in their curriculum provision for all pupils and trainees at all levels in the education system, including the pre-service training of teachers

- must implement their equality and diversity policies from a whole-school or whole-organisation standpoint

- must challenge racism, bias and discrimination in all their forms

- must continuously review and evaluate (through WSE and other evaluation mechanisms) their policies to reflect the population their institutions serve.

The Teaching Council should require colleges of education and education departments in universities that train educators to include compulsory components of equality and diversity training in all their training modules.

The Department of Education and Science, through its Teacher Education Section, the VTST, SDPI, SLSS, PCSP, Leadership Development for Schools, HSCL and education centres, have an essential role to play in the provision of equality and diversity training. It is important that the department's own inspectors continue to receive training in equality and diversity issues in order to upgrade their skills, not only for WSEs but also as they carry out subject and thematic evaluations.

A high priority should be given to the provision of training to the primary sector in the short term, now that the *Guidelines on Traveller Education in Primary Schools* (2002) and the NCCA's *Guidelines on Intercultural Education in Primary Schools* (2005) are both available.

Provision of information
Travellers should have access to information on all aspects of education in a form that is accessible to them. With this information they should be enabled to participate in education, interact with education providers, understand different education provision (such as assessment by NEPS and aspects of the post-primary curriculum and its different programmes), and realise the long-term gains that will accrue to them and their children from involvement in an education system that allows choice for Travellers.

Neither Travellers nor education providers should presume that they understand each other's needs. Effective and open communication that is respectful of both parties has to be built up over time.

Guidance and empowerment
Travellers at all stages in the lifelong education and learning system, from primary to post-primary transition and into further and higher education, require advice and guidance on available options to enable them to make informed decisions. Guidance professionals should be trained to have an understanding and awareness of the particular needs of Travellers and be skilled in enabling Travellers to become involved.

Inclusive, integrated provision
Travellers seek to have their education from pre-school onwards available within an integrated provision that welcomes them as equal participants and also respects their culture. Based on consultations with the partners, a plan for the phased transition from segregated to integrated provision needs to be prepared. However, it is important to be aware that some affirmative targeted initiatives may also be needed to cater for groups of Travellers with specific educational needs. As the transition happens, the resources now provided for segregated Traveller education should be used to implement many of the recommendations in this report, such as the provision of information, training, etc. However, there will still be a need for some targeted initiatives. For example, short-term initiatives may be needed to build capacity within marginalised communities so that they can develop the confidence and knowledge to enable them to engage with mainstream providers.

Review existing provision for Travellers in education
With a view to creating an inclusive education, the provision of Traveller-specific initiatives, such as VTST, RTTs, enhanced capitation, ex-quota hours, and senior Traveller training centres, should be reviewed to determine the best way of providing resources to Travellers involved in mainstream education who have identified educational needs. Educational needs rather than Traveller identity should be the criterion in the provision of additional educational resources to Travellers.

Gender
Affirmative action may be needed to deal with particular aspects of Traveller education as it relates to adult male or female Travellers.

Disability

Travellers with disabilities should be treated in an inclusive environment and in a manner similar to their peers from the settled community who also have disabilities. The providers of such services need to be trained to be sensitive to the particular needs of Travellers.

3. Provision - Equity of access

Travellers should have equity of access. Enrolment policies and practices must be specific about their rights to access. If there are issues concerning enrolment they should be challenged and appealed.

Evaluation

An evaluation and review of provision is necessary in all sectors and aspects of education. For this to succeed it is imperative that the progress of Travellers in education be regularly reviewed and evaluated. The STEP report is welcome and should be regarded as a baseline from which future progress is measured. A second survey should be carried out in approximately five years' time to determine what progress has been made and to inform the review of the strategy. The whole-school evaluation process has a vital role to play in ensuring that school plans, enrolment and other policies as they relate to Traveller primary and post-primary education are formally evaluated. Other evaluation and review mechanisms will be required in the other sectors.

4. Recognition - Needs, not identity, should trigger additional resources

Travellers do not require assistance just because of their identity. As with all other learners, they want special assistance where an educational need has been identified. They also want jobs, either in their own traditional self-employment sector (but recognised and respected by the settled community) or in the mainstream sector based on their qualifications and skills. They do not want such positions placed in jeopardy because of their identity. Travellers want their identity and culture openly respected and acknowledged. They should not have to hide their identity.

Nomadism

At present there are Travellers who are nomadic all the year round and others who are nomadic seasonally. Some Travellers are transient because of accommodation issues. Issues that are specific to nomadic Travellers need to be addressed. Nomadic children need to have a designated base school and appropriate educational supports. Distance learning, through advances in technology, provides new options for providing children with an uninterrupted education. Such an approach needs to be considered within the context of existing provision. The department needs to have a response mechanism for assisting schools where children, including nomadic children, enrol during the academic year.

Data

Data, in an agreed format that is acceptable to Travellers, should be collected to ensure that the progress of Travellers throughout the education system is tracked, that targets for participation are set, and that appropriate resources are then made available. Where the educational outcome is not reached it should be possible to identify these immediately so that appropriate culturally sensitive interventions can be made.

5. Participation - Partnership

Travellers should have equality of participation as pupils and as employees. There should be meaningful partnership between the providers and the participants. In particular, from pre-school to post-primary school the parents of participants should be active partners in decision-making about provision. Traveller pupils should be consulted and their views sought about the most appropriate ways of providing them with a relevant education throughout the spectrum of provision.

Travellers should be encouraged and welcomed to continue to become involved in all aspects of the education system, including involvement in homework clubs, becoming employed as teachers, child-care workers, guidance counsellors, and community education workers, and volunteering to become members of educational structures, such as boards of management. This may involve the provision of specific initiatives to train and enable Travellers to become involved in the education system.

Mentoring

Travellers who have been successful in the education system should be encouraged to act as mentors or role models for other Traveller participants.

High expectations

Because historically many Travellers have had negative experiences of education, an active approach will be needed by the Department of Education and Science, VTST, HSCL, Traveller Organisations, schools and others to convince Travellers that their high expectations from education, both for themselves and for their children, can be realised. Travellers should be involved in the full spectrum of education and not become "niched" in narrow specialisms. They should have educational ambitions and expected outcomes similar to those of their peers in the settled community. All education providers should have high expectations for the outcome of their Traveller pupils.

Inclusion
It is important that segregated provision be phased out, in a planned manner. Other identified issues, such as poor attendance, low attainment levels and poor retention in post-primary school, should be given priority, targets should be set and positive action taken so that future outcomes can be much improved. Travellers have a right to an inclusive mainstream education, but they also have responsibilities as parents in ensuring that their children attend regularly and in encouraging them to achieve to the best of their ability.

11.10 Leadership: the key to success

The successful implementation of the recommendations in this report will happen only if positive leadership from the Government, different departments - particularly the Department of Education and Science - and agencies, policy-makers, boards of management, trustees, patrons, others in management, education providers, the Traveller organisations and the Traveller community is real and not aspirational. All leaders should play a positive role in creating an inclusive environment within their remit that welcomes diversity in all its manifestations. Policies of equality and diversity should be created, but it is their implementation and regular review by all the partners that is vital for the successful changeover to the inclusive environment, whether in a pre-school or in a college of further education.

Everyone in the education system - providers and participants - has rights, but they also have responsibilities, many of which are now enshrined in legislation. Respect for culture is a two-way process. With regard to Traveller education, the majority community must respect and acknowledge Traveller culture. Reciprocally, Travellers must respect and acknowledge the many cultures that are now an integral part of life in Ireland.

The successful implementation of the recommendations in the report will require the effective and successful co-ordination of all aspects simultaneously. Such an approach will create the changed climate in which an inclusive education is available to all in Ireland, including the Traveller community. The implementation of the recommendations in this report, if approved, will take place almost concurrently with the implementation of *Delivering Equality of Opportunity in Schools: An Action*

Plan for Educational Inclusion (2005). The implementation of these two major initiatives should be undertaken in a complementary manner.

11.10.1 Structures
Two high-level officials, one from the administrative side and one from the Inspectorate, should be designated to co-ordinate Traveller education as part of their work. The NEOT should continue to work in promoting the policies of the Department of Education and Science on Traveller education at all levels, with a particular emphasis on inclusion and integration, collaborate with the Teacher Education Section of the Department of Education and Science on the CPD of teachers, and support the implementation of the recommendations when they are approved. The work of the NEOT should be reviewed as part of the general review being suggested for the fourth year of the five-year life span.

The Department of Education and Science's Internal Co-ordinating Committee for Traveller Education should be reconvened to oversee the implementation of the recommendations in this report.

The ACTE should continue to advise the Minister and evaluate the progress of Traveller education as the strategy is being implemented. A representative (or representatives) of the Co-ordinating Committee and the EDC should be co-opted to the ACTE.

11.10.2 Resources
The report recommends that a number of the Traveller-specific provisions be reviewed to determine the best way forward. This could be done under the umbrella of one review that considers the different Traveller-specific provisions. Following the reviews of existing services and resources, it may be necessary to reallocate the Traveller-specific resources. Such resources should be made secure and used to implement the recommendations in this report. Additional resources may also be needed. These will be identified when the implementation plan is prepared.

11.10.3 Implementation of the Traveller education strategy
Following approval of the recommendations in this report by the Minister, the Department of Education and Science should take a leading role in preparing an implementation plan that will activate the strategy. Such a plan would specify which sections of the department and other organisations would be responsible for implementing the different recommendations. The implementation plan would also examine the cost of implementing the different recommendations.

Effective implementation will be determined by the willingness of education providers, of Travellers and

Traveller organisations and of the settled community to work together to change attitudes so that an inclusive, high-quality education is available to all.

At the end of the fourth year it is recommended that a review and evaluation of the strategy be undertaken. This should be done in consultation with all the partners. A further Survey of Traveller Education Provision should be conducted to determine what progress has been made. A national conference on Traveller education should also be convened, which would provide the foundations for the next phase in the development of appropriate responses to the educational needs of Travellers.

Summary of vision for Travellers in 2010
Travellers will:

• obtain access to all mainstream provision

• participate as equals, achieve their full potential, and have outcomes similar to those of their settled peers

• be participants in an education that is changing and evolving into an inclusive system

• gain qualifications, obtain access to mainstream employment, aspire to promotion and participate fully as members of society

• live in suitable accommodation and have health characteristics similar to those of the settled community

• respect and be respected for their culture and identity in an Ireland where diversity, equality and interculturalism are the norm and reciprocally respect other cultures and identities

• contribute to Ireland's social, cultural and economic development.

References

City of Dublin Vocational Education Committee, Pavee Point, and Roma Support Group, *Roma Educational Needs in Ireland: Context and Challenges,* Dublin: CDVEC, Pavee Point, and Roma Support Group, 2005.

Council of Europe, *Framework Convention for the Protection of National Minorities,* Strasbourg: Council of Europe, 1998.

Department of Education and Science, *Chief Inspector's Report, 2001-2004,* Dublin: Department of Education and Science, 2005.

Department of Education and Science, Circular 7/99 (1999): Applications for Posts of Resource Teacher for Children of the Travelling Community.

Department of Education and Science, Circular M43/99 (1999): Support for Post-Primary Schools Enrolling Traveller Children.

Department of Education and Science, Circular 24/03 (2003): Allocation of Resources for Pupils with Special Educational Needs in National Schools.

Department of Education and Science, *Delivering Equality of Opportunity in Schools: An Action Plan for Educational Inclusion,* Dublin: Department of Education and Science, 2005.

Department of Education and Science, *Guidelines on Traveller Education in Primary Schools,* Dublin: Department of Education and Science, 2002.

Department of Education and Science, *Guidelines on Traveller Education in Second-Level Schools,* Dublin: Department of Education and Science, 2002.

Department of Education and Science, *Learning Support Guidelines (for Primary Schools),* Dublin: Department of Education and Science, 2000.

Department of Education and Science, *Literacy and Numeracy in Disadvantaged Schools: Challenges for Teachers and Learners,* Dublin: Department of Education and Science, 2005.

Department of Education and Science, *Pre-Schools for Travellers: National Evaluation Report,* Dublin: Department of Education and Science, 2003.

Department of Education and Science, *Report of the Action Group on Access to Third Level Education,* Dublin: Department of Education and Science, 2001.

Department of Education and Science, *Survey of Traveller Education Provision,* Dublin: Department of Education and Science, 2006.

Department of Education and Science, *White Paper on Adult Education: Learning for Life,* Dublin: Stationery Office, 2000.

Department of Education and Science, *White Paper on Early Childhood Education: Ready to Learn,* Dublin: Stationery Office, 1999.

Department of Education and Science and Equality Authority, *Schools and the Equal Status Acts* (second edition), Dublin: Department of Education and Science, 2005.

Department of Health and Children, *Traveller Health: A National Strategy, 2002-2005,* Dublin: Stationery Office, 2002.

Department of Justice, Equality and Law Reform, *First Progress Report of the Committee to Monitor and Co-ordinate the Implementation of the Recommendations of the Task Force on the Travelling Community,* Dublin: Stationery Office, 2000.

Department of Justice, Equality and Law Reform, *National Action Plan Against Racism: Planning for Diversity,* Dublin: Department of Justice, Equality and Law Reform, 2005.

Department of Justice, Equality and Law Reform, *Report of the Task Force on the Travelling Community,* Dublin: Stationery Office, 1995.

Department of Justice, Equality and Law Reform, *Second Progress Report of the Committee to Monitor and Co-ordinate the Implementation of the Recommendations of the Task Force on the Travelling Community,* Dublin: Department of Justice, Equality and Law Reform, 2005.

Economic and Social Research Institute and National Council for Curriculum and Assessment, *Moving Up: The Experiences of First-Year Students in Post-Primary Education,* Dublin: ESRI and NCCA, 2004.

Education (Welfare) Act (2000).

Education Act (1998).

Education for Persons with Special Educational Needs Act (2004).

Eivers, Emer, Shiel, Gerry, and Shortt, Fionnuala, *Reading Literacy in Disadvantaged Primary Schools,* Dublin: Educational Research Centre, 2004.

Employment Equality Act (1998).

Employment Equality Act (2004).

Equal Status Act (2000).

Equality Act (2004).

Equality Authority, Diversity at School, Dublin: Equality Authority, 2004.

Equality Authority, *Travellers' Experience of Labour Market Programmes: Barriers to Access and Participation,* Dublin: Equality Authority, 2003.

Eurydice, *Integrating Immigrant Children into Schools in Europe,* Brussels: Eurydice, 2004.

Gormally, Eleanor, *Whiddin to the Gauras: Talking to Our Own: Traveller Researchers Talk to Limerick Traveller Children,* Dublin: Veritas, 2005.

Government of Ireland, *Convention on the Elimination of All Forms of Racial Discrimination: First National Report by Ireland on the Convention,* Dublin: Stationery Office, 2004.

Government of Ireland, *First National Report on the Framework Convention for the Protection of National Minorities,* Dublin: Stationery Office, 2001.

Government of Ireland, *National Action Plan against Poverty and Social Inclusion, 2001-2003,* Dublin: Stationery Office, 2001.

Government of Ireland, *National Action Plan against Poverty and Social Exclusion, 2003-2005,* Dublin: Stationery Office, 2003.

Government of Ireland, *Second National Report on the Framework Convention for the Protection of National Minorities,* Dublin: Stationery Office, 2005.

Government of Ireland, *The National Youth Work Development Plan, 2003-2007,* Dublin: Stationery Office, 2003.

Griffin, Gerard, *An Evaluation of Operational Aspects of Senior Traveller Training Centres,* Dublin: National Co-ordinating Unit for Senior Traveller Training Centres, 1998.

Higher Education Equality Unit, *Creating an Inter-Cultural Campus,* Dublin: Department of Education and Science, 2002.

High-Level Group on Traveller Issues Report, Dublin: Stationery Office, 2006.

Housing (Miscellaneous Provisions) Act (2002).

Housing (Traveller Accommodation) Act (1998).

Irish National Teachers' Organisation and Equality Authority, *The Inclusive School*, Dublin: INTO and Equality Authority, 2004.

Irish Traveller Movement, *Moving On: Travellers and Third-Level Education* (video), Dublin: Irish Traveller Movement, 2004.

Kett, Mary, and Morgan, Mark, *The Prison Adult Literacy Survey: Results and Implications,* Dublin: Irish Prison Service, 2003.

Mary Immaculate College, *Achieving Equity of Access to Higher Education in Ireland: The Case of Travellers,* Limerick: Mary Immaculate College, 2005.

National Adult Literacy Agency, *Working Together: Approaches to Family Literacy,* Dublin: National Adult Literacy Agency, 2004.

National Children's Office, *Young Voices: How to Involve Children and Young People in Your Work,* Dublin: National Children's Office, 2005.

National Council for Curriculum and Assessment, *Guidelines on Intercultural Education in the Primary School,* Dublin: NCCA, 2005.

National Council for Curriculum and Assessment, *Towards a Framework for Early Learning,* Dublin: NCCA, 2004.

National Council for Curriculum and Assessment, *Towards a Framework for Early Learning: Final Consultation Report,* Dublin: NCCA, 2005.

National Economic and Social Council, *The Developmental Welfare State (Report 113),* Dublin: NESC, 2005.

National Economic and Social Forum, *A Strategic Policy Framework for Equality Issues* (Forum Report 23): Dublin: NESF, 2002.

National Office for Equity of Access to Higher Education, *Achieving Equity of Access to Higher Education in Ireland: Action Plan, 2005-2007,* Dublin: National Office for Equity of Access to Higher Education, 2004.

National Office for Equity of Access to Higher Education, *Towards a National Strategy: Initial Review of HEA Targeted Initiatives to Widen Access to Higher Education,* Dublin: National Office for Equity of Access to Higher Education, 2004.

National Qualifications Authority of Ireland, *The National Framework of Qualifications,* Dublin: National Qualifications Authority of Ireland, 2003.

Organisation for Economic Co-operation and Development, *Thematic Review of Early Childhood Education and Care Policy in Ireland,* Paris: OECD, 2004.

Pavee Point, *Bridges to the Future: A Report on Future Roles for the Senior Traveller Training Centres,* Dublin: Pavee Point, 1999.

Pavee Point, *Éist: Respecting Diversity in Early Childhood Care, Education and Training,* Dublin: Pavee Point, 2001.

Rottman, David B., Tussing, A. Dale, and Wiley, Miriam M., *Population Structure and Living Circumstances of Irish Travellers: Results from the 1981 Census of Traveller Families,* Dublin: Economic and Social Research Institute, 1986.

Scottish Traveller Education Programme, *Inclusive Educational Approaches for Gypsies and Travellers within the Context of Interrupted Learning: Guidance for Local Authorities and Schools,* Edinburgh: STEP, 2003.

Supporting Equity in Higher Education: A Report to the Minister for Education and Science, 2003.

United Nations, *Convention on the Elimination of All Forms of Racial Discrimination,* New York: United Nations, 1968.

United Nations, *Convention on the Rights of the Child,* New York: United Nations, 1989.

Universities Act (1997).

Youth Work Act (2001).

Appendices

Appendix 1

Abbreviations used in this report

ACTE: Advisory Committee on Traveller Education

AEGI: Adult Education Guidance Initiative

ASSET: After-School Support Educational Training

BTEI: Back-to-Education Initiative

CDVEC: City of Dublin Vocational Education Committee

CECDE: Centre for Early Childhood Development and Education

CPD: continuing professional development

CSO: Central Statistics Office

CWO: community welfare officer

DCU: Dublin City University

DEIS: Delivering Equality of Opportunity in Schools

DES: Department of Education and Science

EDC: Educational Disadvantage Committee

ERC: Educational Research Centre

ESRI: Economic and Social Research Institute

ESRU: Evaluation, Support and Research Unit

EWO: education welfare officer

EYDU: Early Years Development Unit

FÁS: Foras Áiseanna Saothair (Training and Employment Authority)

FETAC: Further Education and Training Awards Council

HEA: Higher Education Authority

HSCL: home-school-community liaison

HSE: Health Service Executive

IBEC: Irish Business and Employers' Confederation

ICT: information and communications technology

ICTU: Irish Congress of Trade Unions

INTO: Irish National Teachers' Organisation

ITM: Irish Traveller Movement

IVEA: Irish Vocational Education Association

JCSP: Junior Certificate School Programme

LCA: Leaving Certificate - Applied

LCVP: Leaving Certificate Vocational Programme

LSTS: Learning Support Teachers

LYNS: Learning for Young International Students (a JMB and ACCS initiative)

NALA: National Adult Literacy Agency

NATC: National Association of Traveller Centres

NCCA: National Council for Curriculum and Assessment

NCSE: National Council for Special Education

NEOT: National Education Officer for Travellers

NEPS: National Educational Psychological Service

NESC: National Economic and Social Council

NESF: National Economic and Social Forum

NEWB: National Educational Welfare Board

NGO: non-governmental organisation

NPC: National Parents' Council

NQAI: National Qualifications Authority of Ireland

NUIC: National University of Ireland, Cork

NUID: National University of Ireland, Dublin

NUIG: National University of Ireland, Galway

NUIM: National University of Ireland, Maynooth

OECD: Organisation for Economic Co-operation and Development

PCSP: Primary Curriculum Support Programme

PLC: post-Leaving Certificate

RCSI: Royal College of Surgeons - Ireland

RTT: resource teacher for Travellers

SCP: School Completion Programme

SDPI: School Development Planning Initiative

SENO: special education needs officer

SLSS: Second-Level Support Service.

SSP: School Support Programme

SSVP: Society of St Vincent de Paul

STEP: Survey of Traveller Education Provision

STTC: senior Traveller training centres

VEC: Vocational Education Committee

VTOS: Vocational Training Opportunity Scheme

VTST: Visiting Teacher Service for Travellers

VTT: visiting teacher for Travellers

WSE: whole-school evaluation

WTE: whole-time equivalent

Appendix 2

Membership of the Joint Working Group

Chairperson
Seán McNamara

Association of Secondary Teachers, Ireland
Moira Leydon

Department of Education and Science
Breda Naughton
Catriona O'Brien
Maugie Francis
Séamus McLoughlin
Gerard Griffin (also from STTC)
Anne Donnellan (VTST)
Rosemarie Taylor (VTST)

Education Disadvantage Committee
Rita Conway
Maura Grant

Irish National Teachers' Organisation
Tom O'Sullivan

Irish Traveller Movement
Catherine Joyce
Cristina Hurson
Damien Walshe
Caroline Doyle
Maureen Ward
Thomas McCann (one meeting)

National Traveller Women's Forum
Ciara Shanahan
Maria Joyce
Cathryn Mannion

Pavee Point
Jane Rooney
Rosaleen McDonagh
Colette Murray
Gearóid Ó Riain (initially representing Pavee Point, then
the external resource person)
Patrick Nevin (one meeting)
Martin Collins (one meeting)

Research officer (November 2003 to March 2005)
Gearóid Ó Riain

**Secretariat of Secondary Schools and Joint
Managerial Body**
John G. Davin

Teachers' Union of Ireland
Declan Glynn

Secretaries to JWG
Olivia Murray
Cathal Wynne

Appendix 3

Membership of the Advisory Committee on Traveller Education
(October 2005)

Chairperson
Gabriel Harrison (Department of Education and Science)

Association of Community and Comprehensive Schools
Michael Meade

Association of Secondary Teachers, Ireland
Sheila Parsons

Catholic Primary School Managers' Association
Name to be provided

Department of Education and Science
Breda Naughton
Catriona O'Brien
Michael Travers
Rhona McSweeney
Mary Horan
Maugie Francis
Gerard Griffin (also representing STTC)
Anne Donnellan (VTST)

Department of Justice, Equality and Law Reform
Brendan Sheehy

Irish National Teachers' Organisation
Tom O'Sullivan

Irish Traveller Movement
Catherine Joyce
Damien Walshe
Cristina Hurson

Irish Vocational Education Association
Philip Cribben

National Association of Traveller Centres
James O'Leary

National Council for Curriculum and Assessment
Majella O'Shea

National Parents' Council - Primary
Francis Linden

National Travellers Women's Forum
Maria Joyce
Cathryn Mannion

Pavee Point
Jane Rooney
Rosaleen McDonagh

Secretariat of Secondary Schools and Joint Managerial Body
John G. Davin

Teachers' Union of Ireland
Declan Glynn

Secretary to committee
Olivia Murray

Appendix 4

Respondents to the consultation process

1. TCD (Trinity College, Dublin) Access Project

2. LINK Project, Tralee

3. Sacred Heart School, Tullamore

4. South Kerry Development Partnership

5. Brian Bradley

6. Tomás Mac Giollachomáin

7. Senior Traveller Training Centres

8. National Consultative Committee on Racism and Interculturalism

9. Scoil Réalta na Maidine, Listowel

10. Exchange House Traveller Service

11. Irish Society for the Prevention of Cruelty to Children

12. St Joseph's Primary School, New Ross

13. Crosscare

14. Kerry Education Services

15. Longford Traveller Movement and Primary Health Care Project

16. Scoil Mhuire, Coolcots, Wexford

17. Mercy Secondary School, Waterford

18. Traveller Health Unit, Midland Health Board

19. National Disability Authority

20. St Brigid's Senior Girls' National School, Finglas, Dublin

21. Galway-Mayo Institute of Technology

22. Our Lady of Fatima National School, Barntown, Wexford

23. Moving On Project, Mary Immaculate College, Limerick

24. Sister Rosarie Martin, Athy Travellers' Club

25. Centre for Early Childhood Development and Education

26. Irish Association of Teachers in Special Education

27. Irish Council for Civil Liberties

28. Traveller Visibility Group, Cork

29. Clondalkin Traveller Development Group

30. St Anne's, Rathkeale, Co. Limerick

31. Presentation Centre for Policy and Systematic Change

32. Limerick Travellers' Development Group

33. Irish National Teachers' Organisation

34. National Association of Travellers' Centres

35. ARD Research

36. St Thomas' Senior School, Dublin

37. Educational Disadvantage Centre, St Patrick's College, Dublin

38. Association of Secondary Teachers, Ireland

39. Youthreach

40. Equality Authority

41. Visiting Teacher Service for Travellers

42. National Traveller Women's Forum

43. National Educational Welfare Board